DESTINY and GREATNESS

THE TWO MOST WANTED

Tarupiwa Muzah

Copyright © 2016. All rights reserved.
No part of this publication may be reproduced, stored in a retrieval system or transmitted in any way by any means, electronic, mechanical, photocopy, recording or otherwise, without the prior permission of the author except as provided by USA copyright law.

All characters appearing in this work are fictitious. Any resemblance to real persons, living or dead, is purely coincidental.

The opinions expressed by the author are not necessarily those of Revival Waves of Glory Books & Publishing.

Published by Revival Waves of Glory Books & Publishing
PO Box 596| Litchfield, Illinois 62056 USA
www.revivalwavesofgloryministries.com

Revival Waves of Glory Books & Publishing is committed to excellence in the publishing industry.

Book design Copyright © 2016 by Revival Waves of Glory Books & Publishing. All rights reserved.

Published in the United States of America

Paperback: 978-1-68411-075-9

Dedication

To my mom Mrs. Rose Muzah, you are an inspiration, thanks

Contents

CHAPTER 1: 7 Destiny Rises 1

CHAPTER 2: 7 C's To Your Impact & Destiny 12

CHAPTER 3: Love Brings You To Your Divine Destiny 22

CHAPTER 4: Hide-Hiding In Weakness Then Exalted In Strength 47

CHAPTER 5: What Makes Greatness 78

CHAPTER 6: Your Greatness Is In 7 Work Environments [I.T.H.R.I.V.E] 89

CHAPTER 7: The Global View—Walking With God Is Raising The Standards 94

CHAPTER 1

7 DESTINY RISES

[ACTION STEPS]

--Make a list of potential partners to help you in your endeavor. [Rise besides]

--Get their contact details and phone numbers, call them and tell them your idea

--Check and see if you are accountable to anyone lately, make a list of those leaders, on each leader check the instruction you have to obey, and tick when making progress. [Rise beneath]

--Write down how much you want to spend on giving, on a monthly basis, and make a list of the people you want to bless, be it in monetary terms or just motivation, and then check your progress. [Rise without]

1. RISE ABOVE   [BACKGROUND]

You can't let your background hinder you from entering your destiny. So you have to rise above it. It's not about where you come from; it's about where you are going. Your background may stop you if you are not careful.

You must see yourself as God sees you. Don't look at what you have now and conclude based on that; that's not your destiny. Rise above that. Look at God's promise in the word, see yourself as the child of the Most High God and go for gold. Go for the fulfillment of your purpose.

When we look in the Bible, we see David, who rose above his background. He was coming from a place of tending the sheep, and rose to the place of prominence when he became the King of Israel.

1 SAMUEL 16 verse 11

So he asked Jesse, Are these all the sons you have? There is still the youngest, Jesse answered; but he is tending the sheep, Samuel said, send for him we will not sit down, until he arrives. Then the Lord said, Rise and anoint him; he is the one.

So we see that it's not about the background for you to enter your destiny, it's about being chosen by God. God looks on the heart; he does not choose you because of where you come from. He makes you to rise from that mud place and makes you sit with the Kings. This is because he delights in you, his most precious creation.

1 SAMUEL 2 verse 8

He raises the poor from the dust, and lifts the needy from the ash heap; he sits them with Princes and has them inherit a throne of honor. For the foundations of the earth are the Lord's, upon them, he has set the world.

Don't look at yourself with the eyes of your background, no, you are born in the image of God. You came from above, not bellow. We look at Jesus Christ; we see that he was born in a manger, from a poor place, but that couldn't stop him. He rose to become the King of Kings. Someone even asked, saying, what good thing can come out of Nazareth? But we see him, Jesus, coming from such a small place, and becoming the King of the Jews.

What you have inside of you is greater than your place of birth. It is greater than your poor background; it is treasured. You must learn to release it without considering yourself or where you are coming from. This will make you to enter your destiny. Go for it, do it, shine the light even without the money.

Don't let it stop you. Peter and John said silver and gold we do not have, but what we have we give you, in the name of Jesus, Rise up and walk, and a miracle took place. They focused on what they had; it was greater than their poor background.

2. RISE BEYOND [THE LIMITS]

You must rise beyond the limitations. You must not be limited. You determine how far you can go. Look afar, set your goals so high, far away for what seems impossible, and you might shock yourself as you realize that you are powerful, as you see those goals being achieved.

You can go as far as you can imagine. There are people who try to limit you, and say you can't go that far, but you must not listen to them. Listen to the word that says Go for it. Don't fear; fear can hinder you to try different things, to progress to different territories as you go for your destiny. Have the courage to stand and say; I will rise beyond the limitation, which comes from me and that others set for me.

We can look at the Bible; we see the story of Moses and the Israelites. Pharaoh said go. But don't go that far. That was a limitation. But we see Moses refusing, saying, No, we must go far with all our belongings. He knew exactly where he was set to go, and could not be stopped.

EXODUS 8 verse 28

Pharaoh said, I will let you go to offer sacrifices to the Lord your God in the desert, but you must not go very far.

But we see that these people of God couldn't be limited because they knew the promise of God. So you must be clear on where you want to go. You must know exactly what you want to achieve from your endeavors. If you are clear, you won't be limited, and you will not settle for less. When less is presented to you, you won't relax, but you will stretch towards that bigger place. This is because you know what you want.

3. RISE BENEATH [UNDER AUTHORITY]

To rise beneath means to be under authority. This will make you to enter your destiny. You must submit to authority. Be humble, for humility goes before honor. You must be a person who is willing to learn from elders, and to be willing to follow their instructions.

PROVERBS 19 verse 20

Listen to advice and accept instructions, and in the end, you will be wise.

You cannot rise as a lone ranger; you must be under so as to go up there. Look at David in the Bible; we see that he was under the authority of his father, Jesse. He was then instructed to go to his brothers to check for them, and give them some food. As he submitted to authority, he was given the opportunity to fight Goliath, and he won the battle.

If he was not under that authority, that opportunity would not be presented to him. He wouldn't be a hero that he became. So you must be accountable to some other leaders, so that you can rise to your destiny. This will make you to be responsible, and you will later fulfill your destiny.

Love those who are above you, your elders, respect them, for they hold your promotion and your destiny. Learn to be kind to them, and you will see the difference. You are one instruction away from your next big break. So be careful to follow the leadership of those on top.

You can only have authority when you are under authority. Humble yourself and you will be lifted up. Sow the seed of honor, and you will be honored. As you obey the instructions, you are sowing honor, and that honor will come back to you in big measure.

4. RISE BEHIND [PATIENCE]

When you rise behind, it seems like you are slow, but no, you are getting there. It's about patience. Don't be discouraged when you see that you are progressing at a slower pace. As long as you are moving, it's okay. The bad thing is to stay at one place.

The little step you take is leading you to your destiny. Jump today and you will fly tomorrow. Time is passing, and you seem like you are behind, but you must know that you are just in time. It's the right moment for you to enter your destiny. Your end will be greater than your beginning.

ECCLESIASTES 7 verse 8

The end of matter is better than its beginning, and patience is better than pride.

This means you must wait. It will happen, be patient. It will happen in its time. Just prepare yourself. Don't be proud and do shortcuts. A shortcut is the longest way to your destiny. Be patient in spirit, you are growing in character and discipline. You are being developed enough for greater responsibilities associated with your destiny.

It does not happen instantly. It's a step by step process for you to reach your full potential. Don't give up, stay on the track, and in no time you will see yourself achieving your dreams and entering your destiny.

Be filled with the Holy Spirit, and have patience as a fruit of the Spirit

GALATIANS 5 verse 22

But the fruit of the Spirit is love, joy, peace, patience.

If you rise behind, it does not mean you are not rising, YES, you are, so continue to step closer and closer to your destiny.

5. RISE BESIDES   [UNITY]

Take a friend with you to your destiny. Rise besides meaning, rise with someone. You need a helping hand to reach your destiny. You can't do it alone. You must be beside someone. Agree with someone.

AMOS 3 verse 3

Can two people walk together unless they agree?

Walk with someone to your destiny. Have someone of the same attitude with you, who sees your drive and who can encourage you to reach your full potential. Find those people who can help you; who agree with your vision and direction.

No one has achieved something big without any help. Have a friend, be a leader. A leader is someone who takes others with him/her to a place of dreams. When two people agree, miracles happen.

MATHEW 18 verse 19

Again, I tell you that, if two of you on earth agree about anything you ask for, it will be done for you by my Father in Heaven.

God blesses unity. When you unite with someone, a blessing is released.

Look at Paul and Silas in the jail, singing hymns. These two were friends and were in agreement, see what happened. Suddenly an earthquake and the jail foundations were shaken. They got freed from the chains; an angel visited them and told them to come out.

This is the power of friendship and agreement; you will be released to your destiny.

So again I say don't be a lone ranger, Ask for help and be friendly to others, this will catapult you to your destiny. A friend in need is a friend indeed. When you need help from others, don't be rude, but you must kindly ask for it, and you will be given. Some people know more than you know, don't act like you know everything.

Unite with someone, have a friend in your destiny exploits, and you will see the difference. A friend can be a great motivation in your pursuit of excellence. Your friend can see things differently from the way you see, and this helps you to get a different view of your situation as you tackle your objectives.

6. RISE WITHIN   [JOY INSIDE]

Your rising must start inside. You must rise from within, how, by having joy in your heart. Have a heart transformation. You must celebrate your success. Every milestone of achievement, every victory lap needs some sort of celebration, and spice to it, for you to enter your destiny.

We worry too much of the next move, but do we really look and see how far we have gone; God has been so faithful in your life, So please, Rise within, have a joyful and merry heart, it will do you good.

Appreciate the little so that you can be given the bigger things that pertain to your destiny. Enjoy the journey; enjoy your gifting. Say yes to your future, which is being unfolded as you go.

PROVERBS 17 verse 22

A cheerful heart is good medicine, but a crushed spirit dries up the bones.

Be cheerful, it will strengthen you. If you become joyful in your work and enjoy it, you will start doing it with more passion. You will see and take every opportunity. This is because you won't have an attitude of someone being forced to do something, but you will pick an attitude of someone grateful for doing it.

What you are grateful for, is what grows in your life? It all starts from your heart attitude. Rise within, be thankful, rejoice and enjoy what you are currently doing, you will enter your destiny. Sorrow can drain your energy, but joy can make you lip to your destiny. No one will love your product if you don't love it. It's you who is responsible for your own heart's attitude, rise and be happy for yourself and others.

Mind the way you look. Your expression, it can show your expectation. Show a hopeful expression and it can transform your actions.

PROVERBS 15 verse 30

A cheerful look brings joy to the heart

It's easy to frown, but know that it's easy also to smile. It's a matter of choice. Choose to smile and your heart will be affected in a positive way. The feeling of joy comes after the action of a smiling look.

Show all the people who come in contact with you that you have faith, and you are going somewhere; you will surely enter your destiny.

7. RISE WITHOUT [GIVING]

To rise without means you are separating something from you. This is to give something. You must be a giver for you to enter your destiny. Be a lover not a hater. A lover always has something for other people. A lover is not selfish, a lover hopes for the good of others. This is the one who enters his/her destiny.

It's not that easy to separate yourself from something you have; it requires a compassionate heart. It's about your heart for you to rise without. Many people struggle to enter their destinies because of the 'Me attitude'. They don't look and see others' needs, they only want to have & have, not to give out.

The give way is the only way to reach your full potential than the get way.

2 CORINTHIANS 8 verse 12

For if the willingness is there, the gift is acceptable according to what one has, not according to what he does not have.

What do you have for the world? What can you give that can help or benefit others. Think for a moment, not on your needs, but on your seeds. No one has nothing, we all have gifts and ideas that can impact others and help our communities. The Bible says, from the abundance of the heart, the mouth speaks. What comes out comes from your heart.

Speaking is also giving, when you motivate somebody or bless others, you are actually giving.

So, go ahead, and speak something positive to someone, give a compliment, encourage somebody, and you will be rising without. We look at our savior Jesus Christ; he rose without when he gave himself up for us all. He died and rose again on the third day, by his blood; we are now forgiven of our sins. Let's follow his example and die to our selfishness, and give out all we have for the benefit of others.

Take a step of faith and release something, Rise without; give and it shall be given back to you, a good measure, shaken down and running over. The measure you give shall be measured back to you. Impact the World in a positive way- rise without. Many are waiting for your help, your idea, your product, your ministry, your invention, and your work. Do it and you will see the difference.

CHAPTER 2

7 C'S TO YOUR IMPACT & DESTINY

[ACTION STEPS]

--Write down the date and time you are willing to commit to pray about your destiny, stick to it on a weekly basis [Connection]

--Write down the idea or gifting revealed to you in prayer time, and then make a list of those who you know have the resources to help, take contact details of networks, follow up and check progress [Combination]

--Make a list of potential buyers of what you sell, send emails and make sales calls, write down at least 10 ways in which you can give out what is now constructed, be it a product, service, ministry, business or company, then start giving, check progress. [Constitution]

1. CONFESSION [IDENTIFY YOUR PROBLEM]

Firstly, you have to confess, meaning you have to identify your problem, see your need. See what's lacking. Admit that you have a problem. For some, that is the hard part. It takes courage to come to terms with yourself and say, oh, I need help; there is something wrong with me.

For you to get yourself on the journey to your destiny, you need to come to that stage of seeing your weakness. Identify your loss so that you can look for your profit. In spiritual terms, you have to confess your sins to the Father, God, and you will be forgiven. This will make you move to your destiny.

Everything does not start in a good state, but you have to pass through difficulty for you to really concentrate on finding the solution.

GENESIS 1 verse 2

Now the earth was formless and empty.

The earth came from that state of shame, and we see what happened, God began to create. You are in a problematic state, so admit it that all this is wrong, you are in confusion, you don't have an identity, and you don't know your purpose. Don't just live like everything is okay. Be angry, and that is the first step to discovery.

Let's look at Elijah in the Bible,

1 KINGS 19 verse 4-

I have had enough, Lord, he said, Take my life, I am no better than my ancestors

This happened when Elijah was running away from Jezebel, who wanted to kill him. He confessed that he was so fed up with his state. He was afraid of Jezebel. He came to grips with his identity and saw a need of help. He confessed that he was no better because of his fears.

So to enter your destiny, start by being fed up with your state, not just being comfortable. You don't have a product to sell; you have not discovered your purpose. You are just living to survive, and there is fulfillment. Hey, be fed up, be angry, and admit it that it's not okay. That will be a start to the journey to your destiny.

It's about coming to the crossroads. The breaking point is always an appointment to your destiny. If you are happy with what's happening in your life, you will not have the courage to change it. Hate that state, that confusion, that misery, that shame, and you will see the difference.

Confess it, and then it will make you rise to enter your destiny.

2. CONNECTION [GO TO MEET GOD-SOURCE OF SOLUTION]

After you identify your need, you see the problem, and you are fed up with all that; you now have to connect to the source. You have to identify the source of the solution. The earth was formless and void; the solution was with God; the source. He is the Alfa and Omega, the beginning and the end. You were born in the image of God, he knows all about your purpose, and all about your destiny.

All you have to do is getting connected to God. Pray to him, fast and worship him; fellowship with God is what you need. Look at Elijah; he went to the mount of God, to get connected to the source. He got connected to the one who made him for his problem to be solved.

PSALMS 121 verse 1-2

I lift up my eyes to the hills, Where does my help come from? My help comes from the Lord, the maker of Heaven and earth

God is the Maker, he is your creator, so connect to him, and you will enter your destiny. He is your helper. He will reveal the secret things of your destiny, as you fellowship and worship him.

3. CONTINUATION   [FIND OUT WHERE GOD IS]

The problem with many is that they give up so easily, but it's all about continuation. You have to make up your mind, stay in God's presence, so that revelation comes to you. YOU must continue so that you find out where God is. We must serve God willingly and serve others eagerly until we discover the best of ourselves.

You must find where God is, because where God is, that's where your victory is, that's where your success is. There are things that you can do for your own pleasure, but there are things that are meant to be done for the rest of your life. Those important things of a lifetime persevere so that you find them.

It is a blessed endeavor, so stick with the Lord and serve him, stay doing more things, so that you find the one thing with all blessings associated with it. Your purpose will be revealed to you as you continue. Act, act and act, and see where God is. What is best for you comes with much action and service. The will of God is progressive; it comes bit by bit as you try in many ways. Trust in him who has your future in his hands.

1 KINGS 19 verse 11

Then a great and powerful wind tore the mountains apart, and shattered the rocks before the Lord, but the Lord was not in the wind, After the wind there was an earthquake, but the Lord was not in the earthquake, After the earthquake came to a fire, but the Lord was not in the fire, And after the fire came to a gentle whisper, Then a voice said to him, What are you doing here?

This all happened as Elijah continued his stay on the mount, he found where God was; in a still small whisper. So you too can find what really makes you tick as you continue to act, using up the gifting inside of you.

4. COMBINATION [JOIN FORCES]

Okay, now you have discovered your gifting, your purpose, and your life work, as you were continuing to act. So what's next, you now have to build networks. You can't do it alone. Your gift has to match with others who can add value to you, and help you enter your destiny.

IT'S all about joining forces with others in the industry that you are in. Problem is solved through combination. Your idea without the help of others is nothing, but when you combine with others, it becomes something. Look for someone with your best interests at heart. Coordinate with that one in your endeavors. Trust in God, he is faithful; he will lead you to the best connections.

The one who gives you the vision also gives you the provision. God knows the solution. The one who made you to discover your gifting can also make you be connected to someone to help catapult you to your impact;

Let's look at Elijah, we see that God spoke to him, and he gave him a network, and gave him connections for the problem to be solved. The problem only needed him to be in combination.

1 KINGS 19 verse 15

The Lord said to him, Go back the way you came, and go to the Desert of Damascus, when you get there, anoint Hazael King over Aram, also anoint Jehu son of Nimshi, King over Israel, and anoint Elisha son of Shaphat from Abel, Meholah to succeed you as Prophet. Jehu will put to death any that escape the sword of Hazael, and Elisha will put to death any who escape the sword of Jehu.

This meant that these connections were the ones who were going to solve the problem of Jezebel, and all the enemies against Israel. So God made Elijah to be connected with Problem solvers. So as you trust in God, you will be connected with those who want you to succeed in your destiny.

5. CONSTRUCTION [BUILD SOMETHING]

After you network and combine, something will happen. We see a product will come out, that's construction. It comes after you network and connect with helpers in your field of endeavor. Something tangible will result from combining with others that are sent your way by your Father, God.

Construction is building something; it's like having now a company. It's when your idea gets mixed with the one who has the resources. Idea plus resources comes a product or a service. This is how you reach your full potential and enter your destiny. It's when something good comes out of your networks.

PROVERBS 16 verse 9

In his heart, a man plans his course, but the Lord determines his steps.

When you have God as your source of solution, you will discover your gifting through revelation. God will determine your steps. He will lead you to the right connections so that something great is constructed; you will surely enter your destiny. God is leading you all the way; you can make things happen.

Okay, you discovered that you are a great singer, only God can determine your steps, he can lead you to the right Producer, then construction happens. Something tangible, a CD or music disc will come out. This is what we mean by construction. Something of high standards is constructed with the help of others. This is how you enter your destiny and be an impact player.

Let's look at Elijah combined with Elisha, something was being constructed, something tangible. Elisha was being mentored and motivated so that the problem will later be solved. The working together of the two was constructive. It was leading to a desired outcome. So make sure your networks are productive networks. They must lead to the construction of tangible results.

6. CONSTITUTION [THE LAW OF GIVING]

Now you come to the stage where you have to obey the law. Constitution is Policy, its law, it comes after construction. When you now have a company, there is need of policy, how things will happen in your company, the rules of conduct must be laid.

Now in this point of view of you entering your destiny, you have to obey the law of giving. Yes, you have constructed it, something tangible has been built, but you cannot just chill with it, no, give it away. Give it, that product, that service that ministry; this will make you enter your destiny. You can't just have a product, and you don't sell it, that's a no, no.

You have to give it, sell the new you that you discovered, sell your ideas, sell your ministry, and sell your service. That's a blessed endeavor.

PROVERBS 11 verse 26

People curse the man who hoards grain, but blessing crowns him who is willing to sell.

This shows us that those who sell products are blessed too. This is because they are making a contribution to the betterment of the communities. So, go ahead and follow the law of giving, and you will surely be blessed. Don't be afraid of selling, learn to sell, your things to others, this is how you enter your destiny and live a life of impact.

Don't hide your company, don't hide your gifting, no, make it shine like the light, so that many will see it. What did Elijah give? He gave his anointing to Elisha. He said to him, if you see me being taken, a double portion of the anointing will come upon you. It happened; Elisha received the anointing as he witnessed Elijah being taken to Heaven in a whirlwind. So we see later on, the enemies were defeated; the problem got solved through giving, and trusting in God, the source of the Solution.

7. COMPLETION [NOW YOU REACH FULFILLMENT]

This is a state when it finally happens, you reach your destiny, and you come to the fulfillment of your purpose. It comes after giving. You were following the principle; now you enter your destiny. You went to God with your problematic life, your confused self, see what has happened now.

Through God you discovered your gifting, it was revealed to you. He also led you to be connected; he determined your steps, and now you give out and sell the products that came after combination. This is what fulfillment is all about. It's all about living a life that has meaning. It's about living a legacy.

You have come to that stage, thank the Father, he is faithful; thank him from your deepest being. Your success has made God to be glorified. The one, who begins it, is the one who makes it reach completion. Don't begin alone, begin with him, and you will see what happens. He only knows what to do with what he has begun; he makes it reach to a place called there.

This is because he owns it all, it's his own doing. He made the earth not to be a place of chaos, not to be an empty place with darkness, no; he made it to be completed. He made it to be inhabited, to be good, to be finished, and to flourish accordingly.

THIS is the same with you, he did not create you to be confused, abused, tormented, unfulfilled, and No-he had great plans when he created you. He wished and desired to make you reach your destiny.

PHILIPPIANS 1 verse 6

Being confident of this, that he who began a good work in you will carry it on to completion until the day of Christ Jesus.

Our God is a good and faithful God; he has done it with you. You have entered your destiny. You have come to the completion.

CHAPTER 3

LOVE BRINGS YOU TO YOUR DIVINE DESTINY

[Action steps]

---Make a list of the areas that you think needs discipline in your life, make a commitment to accept that discipline, see it as love. [SEE IT]

---Write down the promises of God from the word, and start to declare them three times each day, for the whole month. [SPEAK IT]

---Write down ways in which you can best serve the community, and make a commitment to start acting on it. [GIVE IT]

--Make a list of the service you have been offering lately to your community or neighborhood—write down ways in which you can improve on it, and start doing it, check your progress. [GIVE IT]

1. HAVE IT

Yes for sure, love takes you and brings you to your divine destiny. This is because you were born to love. When you do not love, you are stagnant; you don't move and your life will seem to be meaningless. But when love comes to be part of you, you become new and you will discover you possess more than you ever imagined.

Love makes you to enter your destiny; you will find your purpose and be an impact to the community. So now, how do you have this love? First of all, for you to have this love, you have to know the source of love; where does this love come from. Perhaps your life has been just filled with hate and all the bad stuff. It seems like you were not going anywhere.

You were about to just give up. Now I remind you, don't give up, there is a divine destiny waiting for you to enter it. This destiny will give you joy and satisfaction. This comes only by having love inside of you as the first step for you to enter that destiny. To have love means to have a new heart.

You were so used to being stubborn and taking nothing from no one, now for you to go for love; you need that heart of love.

Proverbs 26 verse 24,

He who hates dissembles with his lips and harbors deceit in his heart; when he speaks graciously believe him not, for there are seven abominations in his heart.

This shows us that it's a heart issue. What is in your heart is what matters the most. Hate starts with the heart. So you have to put love in your heart as the first step for you to enter your destiny. This is because it's all about people, so if your heart is full of hate, there is no movement. Your life is not helping others, so this hinders your progress in life.

Proverbs 22 verse 11,

He who loves the purity of heart and whose speech is gracious will have the King as his friend.

This shows us the need for you to have the purity of heart. This is the love in your heart. It makes you to be a friend of a King. So you see, you need that love in your heart. You have to be pure in heart for you to start to impact people.

People don't want to associate themselves with a person who speaks bad words that discourage. But when you have love in your heart, it makes you to speak positively and to encourage others. This makes you to enter your destiny; people will begin to favor you because of your good attitude.

More opportunities will come your way because of having that love in your heart. We also see that it's not easy to just have this love in your heart or to have the purity of heart on your own, especially when you come from a background of hate, abuse, and violence.

There is a need for you to receive Jesus Christ as your personal savior. This will be the first step for you to have this love and to enter your destiny. When you repent and ask for forgiveness, the blood of Jesus then cleanses you from all your transgressions, you then become a new person with a new heart. This is how you will have the love in your heart as the first step. Your life has become a blessing, not a curse to other people.

Ezekiel 36 verse 26,

A new heart I will give you and a new spirit I will put within you, and I will take out of your flesh the heart of stone and give you a heart of flesh.

If you repent of your sins and confess Jesus Christ as your personal savior, and believe that he died, and rose again on the third day, you become a child of God. He will give you a new heart, and he will take away the heart of stone. You will begin to see yourself being tender-hearted and merciful because Christ is now living in you.

To have Jesus Christ is to have love because he is the source of that love. He is the one that died for our sins as a sacrifice and by his blood; we were forgiven of all our sins. He also gave us eternal life which is life everlasting. This is love.

John 15 verse 13,

Greater love has no man than this, that a man lay down his life for his friends.

Jesus Christ did it; he laid down his life for us to have eternal life. There is no greater love than what he did for us. So for us to have loved, we have to surrender our lives to Jesus Christ, and we will start to be like him, and love others like he loved.

This will lead you to enter your destiny because you will now be always in search of ways to love more to show your changed nature, and doors start to open for you. Confessing Christ Jesus as your savior and believing that he died and rose again on the third day is saying Jesus come into my heart. It's making your heart to be closer to God.

Mathew 15 verse 8,

This people honor me with their lips, but their heart is far from me.

This shows us that there are people who say God did this for me. They speak as if they honor God, but look closely at their actions; you will be surprised. Definitely, you will know by their actions that their hearts are far. To make your heart closer, you have to repent of your sins, be serious about Christ. It's always a heart issue.

When you are now serious, you are having the love inside your heart, and it becomes the first step for you to enter your God-given destiny. Your talk can show what's inside of you, that it's not of love, and this needs to stop.

For you to get out of this trap, you need to let Jesus Christ be the one to help you in changing your heart.

Mathew 15 verse 19,

For out of the heart come evil thoughts, murder, adultery, fornication, theft, false witness, slander.

This all comes from the heart, and also it manifests by the mouth, and all this shows that you don't have love within you. So you ask now saying how I can change my heart so that I can have this love. The answer is that when you confess Jesus Christ as your savior you are surrendering your life to him.

You are following his footsteps; you will learn from him, and you will see yourself reacting to situations like him; this is the new birth.

Mathew 11 verse 29,

Take my yoke upon you, and learn from me, for I am gentle and lowly in heart, and you will find rest for your souls, for my yoke is easy, and my burden is light.

This shows us that you will have a lowly heart as you start believing in the Lord, and you will feel the tension being released from you, the rest comes to you, you become free from that hate attitude that was hindering your progress. This hate was also stopping you from being used by God to help others. We can take the example of Paul in the Bible.

Acts 9 verse 20,

And in the synagogue immediately he proclaimed Jesus saying, 'He is the Son of God'.

We can see in this case a change of heart. This is the violent Saul, who was known for persecuting the Apostles, bringing them bound; now we see a sudden switch. He is now having a heart of flesh. He is now lowly-hearted.

He is now proclaiming that Jesus is the Son of God. This is having love. It comes after believing in Jesus Christ, and you get baptized and filled with the Holy Spirit.

This makes you to have love and be a different person altogether. You will start to live your life with others in mind; you will begin to bless not curse. This is the first step which brings you to your divine destiny.

2. SEE IT

To see love is to change your focus, and this will lead you to enter your destiny. When you now have love, the devil will come to remind you of your past failures. He will remind you of the haste in the past. He wants you to hate yourself for all the bad you have done.

Many people get trapped in this; they feel hopeless. It's all about what you see. You must realize that you are now a new creation, the old has gone, and you have opened a new page of love in your life. You are now committed to Jesus Christ, and all your sins are now forgiven, the moment you accepted Jesus Christ as your personal savior.

Zechariah 3 verse 2-4,

And the Lord said to Satan, O Satan, The Lord who has chosen Jerusalem rebukes you! Is not this a brand plucked from the fire, Now Joshua was standing before the angel, clothed with filthy garments, then the angel said to those who were standing before him, Remove the filthy garments from him, And to him he said, Behold I have taken your iniquity away from you and I will clothe you with rich apparel.

We can see in this situation that what made Joshua to be clothed in filthy garments is what he was focusing his eyes on. He was not seeing love, that he was forgiven, but the Devil was constantly accusing him and making him feel shame for all that happened.

This is a trick of the Devil. You must see love; this means you must focus on what God has done for you, making you to be called a son of God. That is love, see it, believe it, you are now clothed with rich apparel, you are now a son of a King.

See love and for sure you will enter your divine destiny. This is because the way you act and do things is directly proportional to what you see with your own eyes. You must not look at the threats of the enemy, but look at the love of God.

You must see that with this love you are going to reach your full potential. This is because of the grace of the Lord in your life.

1 John 3 verse 1-2,

See what love the Father has given us that we should be called the children of God, and so we are. The reason why the world does not know us is that it did not know him.

This is a command of focus, see means you must focus on the love that the Father has given you. You have that love; now you have to see it. You are now a child of God. This makes you to increase your faith in God. You will know that the one who redeemed you can make you enter your destiny.

He loves you and wants you to make it. Many of the times we make mistakes, and we fall back to that hate, and that madness, but we don't have to give up on our new found love. We have to remember that love when the accuser tries to torment us.

The road is not that easy when you now have love, and you are now a son of God. Things may seem to become even harder when you have accepted Jesus Christ as your savior. You feel alone and discouraged, and you ask yourself saying is this love that I received. When this happens, you have to read the word of the Lord. You must focus your eyes on the promises of God; that's how you start to see the love, and you will be strengthened in your journey.

Psalms 119 verse 82,

My eyes fail with watching for thy promise, I ask, When wilt thou comfort me.

This is David; he had a habit of reading the word of God, waiting on the Lord even when things were hard for him. This made him to be strong, because he was seeing the love, growing his faith, and trusting in God, knowing that it's only God who was going to make him enter his destiny.

Even when problems come your way, you will see them as opportunities for the display of God's love, and you trust him that he is going to show his glory through that situation. This only happens when your eyes are completely saturated in looking at love, searching the scriptures, and knowing the promises of God. You will have a different view of the situation.

When we look at David, we can see that when everyone else was frightened at the sight of Goliath, David was not at all scared. He saw an opportunity, he saw love.

1 Samuel 17 verse 24,

All the men of Israel, when they saw the man, fled from him, and were much afraid.

But we see that David went on to ask more about the benefits to be given to the one who will kill Goliath. When others saw trouble, David saw love. He was more focused on the promise of God that he was going to be King. That became the reason why he did not panic, but believed that God was going to show his glory through him.

We know what happened next. David killed Goliath with a sling and a stone. This made David to be promoted and to enter his destiny.

Psalms 119 verse 148,

My eyes are awake before the watches of the night, that I may meditate upon thy promise.

This shows us that David loved the law of God, and this led him to enter his destiny. For you to enter your divine destiny, you have to see love as a second step. When you do this, you will use the gifts that the Lord gave you through the Holy Spirit without fear of being intimidated by the environment or the threats that surround you.

Psalms 123 verse 1-2,

To thee I lift up my eyes, O thou who art enthroned in the heavens, Behold, as the eyes of the servants look to the hand of their Master, as the eyes of a maid to the hand of her mistress, so our eyes look to the Lord our God, till you have mercy upon us.

This shows us that you have to keep on seeing the love until God has mercy on you and makes you to enter your destiny. You will use your spiritual gifts to impact the community and live your life for others.

When we look at the story of the Israelites, we see that when a group was sent to spy out the land of Canaan, most of the people that were sent saw themselves as grasshoppers compared to the men they saw in the land. It's all about what you see.

If you see love, it shows you believe in God's love, and you don't concentrate on the obstacles on the way to your destiny. Only the two, Joshua and Caleb came with a different report, they saw the love of God, how good the land was.

Numbers 14 verse 7,

[Joshua & Caleb], And said to all the congregation of the people of Israel, The land, which we passed through to spy it out, is an exceedingly good land, if the Lord delights in us, he will bring us into the land and give it to us, a land which flows with milk and honey.

These two saw love; they remembered that they had been redeemed from Egypt, and God loved them. So we see that they didn't look at the threats of the enemy or how big the problem they were encountering was. They focused on the promise of God. God had already made it clear that Canaan was their land, so when they passed by to spy on it, they saw the goodness of God. We see that after all this; Joshua and Caleb were the ones that entered the destiny, and also the children that were born in the wilderness. All the others who saw no love, but were grumbling and complaining did not enter.

To see love also means to follow God's instructions. It is to see it as love, and this most of the time deals with your pride and your ego. God can tell you to stop a habit that seems to be so interesting or nice to you.

To see love in this situation means to see the end result of that command. You have to see that it's for your own benefit. This will make you to enter your divine destiny because as you follow those instructions, the blessings of obedience will follow you, and God will show his glory through you.

Hebrews 12 verse 6,

For the Lord disciplines him whom he loves, and chastises every son whom he receives.

So after you receive Jesus as your savior, that's having love, and it's the first step, then you must also see it as love when God now disciplines you in some areas of your life. God will be now dealing with your character.

It's love; you have to see it that way because at the end it will make you to enter your destiny, and be a blessing to the community. Verse 11 of Hebrews says, For a moment all discipline seems painful rather than pleasant; later it yields the peaceful fruit of righteousness to those who have been trained by it.

So when it happens to you, don't try to fight it, or even decide to go back to your old self. You must just obey and see love in all that, and you will be blessed. When we look at the story of Naaman in the Bible, we see that he was angry when

Elisha told him to go and wash in the Jordan seven times. He did not see the love in that, because he thought that they are better rivers that Elisha could have told him to go to.

2 Kings 3 verse 12,

Are not Abana and Pharpar, the rivers of Damascus, better than all the waters of Israel, could I not wash in them and be clean.

Naaman was suffering from leprosy, and became angry when he was instructed to go and wash in Jordan. He didn't see love, but when his servant told him to just go and do it, he did it and his flesh was restored like the flesh of a little child. This is love; the longing of our Father to restore us back to our original place.

The problem with most of us is that, when God commands them to do this or that, to forgive, to shun evil, we get angry and rebel. This slows us from entering our destinies. All you have to do is to see love, and follow every instruction of God, even when it costs you your reputation, just know that it's the love of God leading you to your restoration.

2 Kings 6 verse 14,

So he went down and dipped himself seven times in the Jordan, according to the word of the man of God; and his flesh was restored like the flesh of a little child, and he was clean.

After following God's commands, and listening to what the Holy Spirit is telling you, miracles happen in your life, and this brings you to your divine destiny. You may have a certain weakness that you know about, you always focus your attention to it, and it lets you down and hinder you from reaching your full potential. But now all you have to do is see the love and ignore the weakness.

You must see God's power to use you even when you are weak in certain areas of your life. We read in the bible the story of Gideon; we see that he did not see love when he considered his background and his weaknesses. All he had to do was to see love, believe in what the angel was saying about him, who he truly was, not the negative things he was focused on.

Judges 6 verse 12,

And the angel of the Lord appeared to him and said to him, The Lord is with you, you mighty man of valor.

We see that Gideon did not see love, but he saw the enemy, the threats, and what the Midianites had done to them. There was a need for him to change his focus for him to enter his divine destiny. He needed to follow the command of God, which says, Go, in that might of yours, and deliver Israel from the hand of the Midianites.

When God gives you a command saying, Go, and do this, that is love. You must see it as love because when he commands, he then passes the authority to bring to pass everything he sends you to do. His grace follows his commands and instructions. So all you need to do is to see that love, and believe that it's already done. You already have the victory.

You don't have to look at your past mistakes, failures or weaknesses, but just to see love. You must see that you are the chosen of the Lord, and he will show his glory through you.

Gideon had it wrong; his eyes were looking at his own weaknesses.

Judges 6 verse 15,

And he said to him, pray, Lord, how can I deliver Israel, Behold my clan is the weakest in Manasseh, and I am the least in my family, but the Lord answered and said, I will be with you, and give you the victory.

At the end, we see that Gideon finally changed his focus, and obeyed the command and instruction without looking at the limitations. He finally saw the love of God; he focused on the words of God, and his promise to give him victory. This made Gideon to enter his divine destiny.

So we see in this situation that what you focus your attention to, can either hinder your progress or accelerate you to your destiny. If you see love, your actions will not be that of a coward, but you will begin to act in faith. You will begin to use the gifting of the Holy Spirit that was put upon you to impact the community without hesitation or looking at your background or weaknesses. This will bring you to your divine destiny. God will use you even when you are weak in other areas of your life.

3. SPEAK IT

Now we have come to the third step; you now have to speak lovingly. I know you were so used to speak negative things about yourself, but you have now repented. Jesus Christ is now your savior, you are now free from the hate, and all the bad things that were hindering your progress. You changed your focus and started to see love in all the situations. Now you have to let that love come out of your mouth.

Proverbs 18 verse 20,

From the fruit of his mouth a man is satisfied; he is satisfied by the yield of his lips.

This shows us the power of speaking. If you speak love, the fruits of love will surround your life, and you will be satisfied with it.

So you have to be careful about the words that you speak. This is because when words come out of your mouth, they make things to exist, they yield fruit. So if its bad words of hate, doubt, unbelief, fear, they make all this to appear in your life, and also in everything that you do. So you have to have a new habit of speaking love towards yourself and others. This will make favor to manifest itself around you, and you will surely enter your divine destiny.

For you have a habit of speaking love, you must worship God for his goodness. Praise and worship must be always part of your daily duties. This is because when you praise and worship the Lord, you are proclaiming his love, and this will make the Lord to visit you. He will give victory to you in your situations.

Isaiah 63 verse 7,

I will recount the steadfast love of the Lord, the praises of the Lord, according to all that the Lord has granted us, and the great goodness to the house of Israel, which he has granted them according to his mercy, according to the abundance of his steadfast love.

When you are praising and worshiping God. You are recounting his love; you are speaking it, according to all that he has done to you. This will open doors for you because it increases your faith. It shows you trust in God, that he will make you to enter your destiny.

Even when situations confront you that seem to be bad, don't be discouraged, but just speak love, and worship God. He will come to your aid, and give you the victory that you need in that situation. We can also see the benefits of speaking love when we look to the story of King Jehoshaphat.

When he was confronted by the three Kings who joined forces to destroy the Israelites, the men of Ammon, Moab, and Mount Seir, King Jehoshaphat spoke love by using the praise and worship as the team to lead the people in the battle.

2 Chronicles 20 verse 21,

And when he had taken counsel with the people, he appointed those who were to sing to the Lord and praise him in holy array, as they went before the army, and say, Give thanks to the Lord, for his steadfast love endures forever.

This shows us that King Jehoshaphat decided that in this situation, we have to just speak the love of God and not look at the threats of the enemy. Praising God and thanking him is speaking his greatness and love. This made the Lord to be pleased with them and they won the victory. Verse 22 says, And when they began to sing and praise, the Lord set an ambush against the men of Ammon, Moab and Mount Seir. These men helped to destroy themselves.

This shows us that you have to speak love, talk about God's goodness and mercy towards your life. You have to sing his praise, and you will see hard situations being softened for you, and this will bring you to your divine destiny. When we look at the story of Job, we can see the power of speaking love and how it brings you to your divine destiny.

Even when Job was tested and was suffering, he kept his integrity; he spoke love instead of hate or doubt. We hear Job saying in Job 19 verse 25, For I know that my Redeemer lives, and at last he will stand upon the earth, and after my skin has been thus destroyed, and then from my flesh I shall see God.

This shows us that Job did not curse God, but spoke love of God when he was at this time of testing and suffering. This made God to be pleased with him, and make him to enter his destiny; He then received double riches than he had at first.

Job 42 verse 7,

After the Lord had spoken these words to Job, the Lord said to Eliphaz, the Temanite, my wrath is kindled against you, and against your two friends, for you have not spoken of me what is right as my servant Job has.

We see in the above verse that Job got blessed because of speaking love, for he spoke what is right before the Lord. Verse 12 says, And the Lord blessed the latter days of Job more than his beginning. This shows us that you have to mind your words. Speak love, speak God's goodness, not the situation; how big or bad it is, or how the enemy has wiped you.

Don't give the enemy an open door to destroy you by your words. If you speak love even when it's not yet manifesting, God will show his glory through you in his time. Continue; don't give in to the trick of the Devil to speak the doubt or bad stuff that comes to your mind.

You may think it but don't speak it. Speak love and this will bring you to your divine destiny.

Hebrews 13 verse 15

Through him then let us continually offer up a sacrifice of praise to God, that is, the fruit of lips that acknowledge his name.

This shows that it must be done continuously, speaking love of God, praising him, and he will surely help you in your time of need. Speaking love and acknowledging his name is pointing to him as the reason for your strength.

Every breakthrough that you receive, you have to say that it's because of the love of God that I have received this. You have to give glory to God for the little achievements that happen to you as you began your journey as a child of God. You accepted Jesus Christ as your savior, and the Holy Spirit came upon you, so you now have the love.

Then now you see your life that it has changed. You are now receiving victory in some areas that you were not having victory before. This is because God is now working with you. So you have to speak love; give glory to God for those small victories. God will then open bigger opportunities for you because you speak his love, and this will bring you to your divine destiny.

We also see that you need to speak the word of the Lord every time, verbalize it, don't just meditate upon it only; this word is the word of love. The Bible is full of promises of God for your life, promises of blessings for the upright. So when you speak the word of God, this word of love which is alive, will cause situations to change for your good. This is because our Lord God watches over his word to fulfill it.

Joshua 1 verse 8,

This book of the law shall not depart out of your mouth, but you shall meditate on it day and night, that you may be careful to do all that is written in it, for then you shall make your way prosperous and then you shall have good success.

This shows us that when you speak this word of love, you will succeed; you will certainly enter your God-given destiny.

4. GIVE IT

1 Corinthians 14 verse 1,

Make love your aim, and earnestly desire the spiritual gifts, especially that you may prophesy.

Verse 3 says, on the other hand, he who prophesies speaks to men for their up building and encouragement and consolation.

This verse shows us that, after you have love as the first step towards your destiny, you are now a child of God, and you ask for the Holy Spirit to come upon you.

When you get filled with the Spirit, you will then come to a stage where you have to give that love to others. This shows us that you must desire to encourage others and give them motivation. This is how you give love, be of service to others and you will enter your destiny. This is because you were born to help others. Your purpose is to benefit other people using the spiritual gifts that were endowed upon you by God.

Giving love to others is true joy and fulfillment. It shows that you are following Jesus Christ your savior, because he came to serve and to give his life as a ransom for our sins.

1 John 3 verse 16-18,

By this we know love, that he laid down his life for us, and we ought to lay down our lives for the brethren, but if anyone has the world's goods and sees his brother in need, yet closes his heart against him, how does God's love abide in him? Little children, let us not love in word or speech, but in deed and in truth.

This shows us that you must give love because you are now a child of God, and you must display the love of God you have received. You must give even the world's goods to your brethren in need, and not just speak love but giving it.

When you do honest service to your brethren, and you use your abilities for the benefit of others, this is giving love. You will reach your full potential and enter your God-given destiny. This is because you are now a giver of love, and God will open avenues for you to give more.

Giving love is taking every opportunity that comes our way to give love to others.

We miss our destiny because of selfishness. God places opportunities of giving, but we focus more on what we are going to get out of it. When it seems like there is no benefit to us, we shun the opportunity, not knowing that God is testing us to see what's in our hearts before he makes us enter our destinies.

This is because God checks our maturity first before any promotion. He will not put you in a leadership position for you to just think of yourself, you won't be useful for that position. You won't be effective enough to do what needs to be done.

When we look at the story of Mordecai in the Bible, we see him giving love to the King, not considering what's going to be given back to him. He just saw an opportunity to give, and he did not hesitate.

Esther 2 verse 21,

And in those days, as Mordecai was sitting at the King's gate, Bigthan and Teresh, two of the King's eunuchs, who guarded the threshold became angry and sought to lay hands on King Ahasuerus, And it came to the knowledge of Mordecai, and he told it to Queen Esther, and Esther told the King in the name of Mordecai.

We see here that Mordecai saw an opportunity to give love, and he did it for the King. He acted and gave love not because there was some benefit that he expected to receive for that action. He was just laying down his life for the brethren.

It was a show off of the love that was in his heart. We know that the same Mordecai had adopted Esther when her parents died; this was also giving love without any benefit in mind. We see that later on, he entered his destiny because of giving love.

The King remembered him, and he was promoted for his actions. This shows us that it's in giving love that you enter your destiny. Mordecai became second in rank to King Ahasuerus. That was his divine destiny.

We see that it was by giving love first to Esther then to the King that made him to enter that destiny.

Luke 6 verse 38,

Give, and it will be given to you; a good measure, pressed down, shaken together, running over, will be put into your lap, for the measure you give will be the measure you get back.

So this means if you give love, love will come back to you a good measure. When you love people, even those ones that hate you, a good measure will come back to you. You will be rewarded by God, and he will make you to enter your destiny. God will open to you bigger doors and give you bigger responsibilities.

When giving love and sacrificing your time for the benefit of others, you don't worry about the payback period. You don't worry about how long it will take before you enter your destiny. All you know is that the more you give love to others, the more God will bless you and increase you to make you a blessing to more people.

When we look at the story of David, we see that when he was anointed to be King, he was given an opportunity to use his gifting of playing the instrument. He was giving love to the King, who had an evil spirit tormenting him, and when he played, the evil spirit would depart from Saul.

1 Samuel 16 verse 21

And David came to Saul, and entered his service, and Saul loved him greatly and he became his armor bearer; and Saul sends to Jesse, saying let David remain in my service, for he has found favor in my sight, and whenever the evil spirit from God was upon Saul, David took the Lyre and played it with his hand; so Saul was refreshed, and was well, and the evil spirit departed from him.

This shows us that David was known for giving love, doing service to the King using his gifting and ability. He did not worry about the payback period of all his services. He knew that another opportunity for more giving of love will be presented by God, and he will surely enter his destiny of becoming the King of Israel.

You must always see the value of giving love. You must know that it's God at work. When God trusts you with little, he is training you for even greater service to the community. How you treasure the little opportunity to give love makes the difference.

You must always place a high value in every little bit of giving love that is presented to you, and know that it's the road to your entering of your destiny. It's always stage by stage. We know that David killed Goliath with a stone and won a great victory for the Israelites, but when we look closely, we see that he valued the little giving love instruction from his father, Jesse.

1 Samuel 17 verse 17,

And Jesse said to David his son, Take for your brothers an ephah of this parched grain, and these ten loaves, and carry them quickly to the camp to your brothers, also take these ten cheeses to the commander of their thousand.

This seemed not so important, but it was carrying a great promotion on David's part. If he treated it lightly, he could have missed the opportunity to take on Goliath. So it means you must always be careful, also be willing to give love to any opportunity no matter how small it is. It could be the one meant for your promotion to your divine destiny.

God works in ways we don't understand sometimes, so be willing and obedient and give love every time. This will bring you to your divine destiny. God bless you.

CHAPTER 4

HIDE-HIDING IN WEAKNESS THEN EXALTED IN STRENGTH

[ACTION STEPS]

---Make a list of the things you want to separate yourself from, also the groups or people you are to disconnect from; this is for your progress in identifying your destiny, check how far you have gone [SEPARATE YOURSELF]

--Write down the things you are willing to do to move on with your life, as you wait, make a plan on how to do it, and get in the action gear [BE SENT]

--Write down the simple and small tasks you are willing to commit to, then start doing it, check your progress. [BE FAITHFUL]

1. Peter [humble yourself]

When we look closely to the story of Peter, we can see that he went on to hide in weakness, he denied Jesus Christ, and later we see him being exalted in strength. He entered his destiny.

We can see that after he denied Jesus Christ three times, he then later received the Holy Spirit and started to boldly testify about Jesus' resurrection.

Mathew 26 verse 6,

Now Peter sat outside in the courtyard, and a maid servant came unto him saying, you also were with Jesus of Galilee, but he denied it before them all, saying I know not what you say, and when he was gone out into the porch, another maidservant saw him, and said unto them that were there ,this fellow was also with Jesus of Nazareth, and again he denied it with an oath, I do not know the man, and after a while came un to him they that stood by, and said to Peter, surely you also are one of them, for your speech betrays you, then began he to curse and to swear, saying, I know not the man, and immediately the cock crowed, and Peter remembered the words of Jesus who said unto him, before the cock crows, you shall deny me three times, and he went out and wept bitterly.

When we look at this story, we can find out that Jesus knew that Peter was going to deny him. So we see that God knows that you are going to hide, he even expects it from you. You have to see yourself as a human with a lot of weaknesses, and then you will discover the need of his love towards you. You have to humble yourself and see the need of his grace.

You have to see that you are a sinner in need of grace, and without God's help, you are bound to fail. Then when you lower yourself, he will come and exalt you in strength. You will certainly enter your destiny.

John 6 verse 6,

For he himself knew exactly what he was to do.

Okay, YES, he knew that he was going to multiply the five loaves and two fish to feed the five thousand, so why did Jesus ask them how to do it. This shows us that God's tendency is to make us see how weak we are without him. He makes us to see our own incapacities, our own humanity, so that he makes us will to be done without our contribution, and shows his divinity.

John 6 verse 7,

Philip answered him Two hundred penny worth of bread is not sufficient for them, that every one of them may take a little, one of his disciples, Andrew, Simon Peter's brother said unto him, there is a lad here who has five barley loaves and two small fishes, but what are there among so many,

Jesus was making them to see their own weakness, so that they decide to hide, and when they do hide, he then instructs them and takes over the matter. God wants full control. He does not want to share his glory with you.

Give him the control; hide yourself in your weakness and in your failure. Acknowledge that you can't do it on your own and leave it all to him. Agree that this is bigger than you. It's God who made you to face such a great situation so that you can know that it's him who can do it through you.

All this time Peter thought he was so great. He even confessed that all other disciples can deny Jesus, but not him. This attitude of thinking that he can do it on his own without God's grace being involved was not going to do him good.

Total dependence is the secret of success in any endeavor of entering your God-given destiny. Peter had to learn this the hard way. A situation came that made him to hide, to see his weakness and to weep bitterly. He came to his senses and saw that he was not involved in his greatness, but God was the one in control. God was going to use a weak man like him to show his glory.

James 4 verse 9-10,

Be afflicted, and mourn, and weep, let your laughter be turned to mourning, and your joy to heaviness, humble yourself in the sight of the Lord, and he shall lift you up.

This verse is saying HIDE, and you will see what happens next. You will be exalted in strength, only when you hide in weakness. Fail yourself and God will not fail you. When we look at great people, we can see that most of them came from a lot of failures, they were hiding in their weaknesses, and we see later God exalts them in strength.

The likes of Apostle Prof Ezekiel Guti, we can see that he went to hide in the bush of Bindura, and later was exalted in strength when he became the founder of Forward in Faith ministries international, the fast growing global Pentecostal church from Africa.

When the Bible says be afflicted, and mourn, it's a command to hide. Why are you being commanded to hide, because there is a benefit you are going to receive. You are going to be exalted in strength. God is going to do it for you, and make you to enter your destiny.

When it looks like failure, God gets pleased by your lowliness, and you see that it becomes a success when he gives you grace. The Bible says he gives more grace. This more grace is given to the humble. Weeping and groaning are sign of humbleness. God hates pride. It's because of pride that the devil is causing havoc in our days.

So as the devil was resisted and cast down to the earth, all his proud friends face the same predicament. So we see that only the humble are now candidates for exaltation in strength. So we see that if you sow in tears, you will reap with joy. Joy will come to you when you reduce yourself and depend entirely upon God. When you see how weak you are on your own, God will then promote you to your destiny.

2. David [be faithful]

The first instance of David hiding in weakness was seen when he was in service to his father. We can see that a command to HIDE is also a command to serve under authority. When you are doing little things of service and you have no title, office or any prestigious position, that's hiding. It's not seeking to be seen by man, but it's just faithful over a little.

It's humble enough to serve. God, then will choose you and exalt you in strength. Then we look closely to the story of David; we can see that when Samuel came to anoint a King from Jesse's house, David was not even called to the feast. He was hiding in the service of keeping the sheep in the wilderness.

It seemed like a failure, but it became a success, when he was noticed, not by man but by God. This shows us that when you hide in service working under the authority in lower positions, God will notice you, and you will then be exalted in strength.

The Bible says those who seek to be seen by man when they give, have already received their reward; our Father sees in secret and he rewards openly. Samuel said surely the Lord's anointed is before me, when Eliab, the elder brother stood in front of him, but God said no, I don't see as you see, I don't notice as you notice. God looks at the heart of service. God, even later testifies, saying, David, a man after my own heart, who will do all my will.

Hiding is seeking to be noticed by God. It is when you do the Will of God faithfully not wanting to be noticed by men. It was in the heart of David to build a temple for God's dwelling. His heart was full of service, that's the reason he got noticed by God, and he was then exalted in strength.

1 Samuel 16 verse 11,

And Samuel said unto Jesse, Are here all your children, And he said, there remains yet the youngest, and behold, he keeps the sheep, and Samuel said unto Jesse, sent and bring him, for we will not sit down till he comes here, and he sent and brought him in, Now he was ruddy, and of a beautiful countenance, and handsome, and the Lord said, Arise, anoint him, for this is he, Then Samuel took the horn of oil and anointed him in the midst of his brethren; and the spirit of the Lord came upon David from that day forward.

David was hiding in weakness. He was weak in the sense that he was the youngest in the family of Jesse. Also just agreeing to keep the sheep of his Father was a form of hiding. He was keeping the few sheep, and then God exalted him to become the King of Israel.

When you are faithful over a little God will open a door for more. The problem with a lot of us, we want to do big things that people can see, but it's about hiding. Serve in the little things first, and then God will notice you and will then exalt you in strength. We can see the even after he was anointed to be King of Israel, David did not immediately declare that I'm now King and try to kill Saul to take the position.

He went back to keeping of sheep. Now we see that this is hiding in weakness. That seems more like a failure, because we can ask, and say, so what's stopping you from being in that position of a King. We see that David was still seeking to be noticed by God not man.

He continued to serve under the authority of his father, and also under Saul. Even when Saul wanted to kill David, he went to hide in the caves. David was so good in this area of hiding in weakness. He knew that it's God who notices and rewards according to faithfulness.

Most of the time people want a title or position more than just being faithful. You have to hide, be faithful over the little tasks you are assigned to, so that God will notice you and exalt you in strength, and you enter your destiny.

1 Samuel 26 verse 23-25,

The Lord render to every man his righteousness and his faithfulness; for the Lord delivered you into my hand today, but I could not stretch forth my hand against the Lord's anointed, and behold, as your life was precious this day in my eyes, so let my life be precious in the eyes of the Lord, and let him deliver me out of all tribulation.

David knew that it was all about being faithful to serve under the King. He talked about God noticing his faithfulness. It seemed like weakness to resist killing Saul so as to take a position, but it was strength.

He left it all to God; that's what hiding is all about. It's about leaving it all to God to see you as you serve in little things faithfully according to his will. Then afterwards God will reward you and exalt you in strength in his own way.

3. John the Baptist [separate yourself]

Before you enter your destiny, you pass through times of loneliness. You have to separate yourself from all others, so that in due time God will exalt you to your uniqueness. You have to get away from comparing yourself to other people, because God wants you to be prepared for your destiny.

To hide in weakness can also mean to be seen by people as nothing, to be insignificant to them according to the society standards. This makes you to be lonely then you hide in that weakness.

When it seems like you can't fit into the normal that the society sets for you, you get lonely, misunderstood, and you hide in that loneliness. It's God who has commanded you to hide; he wants to use your life in a unique way.

Luke 1 verse 80,

And the child grew, and became strong in spirit, and was in the deserts till the day of his showing unto Israel.

This was not a normal experience for John. He went on to hide in the deserts. Even the food he was eating was different from the others. Sometimes loneliness can be associated with weakness. It seems like you can't connect with others, and you feel miserable and depressed.

Sometimes you then try to do like others so that maybe you may fit into their expectations of you, but this message is encouraging you to hide like John the Baptist. Do not worry yourself, and do not try to fit in.

God will show the reason why you were so lonely and could not fit into the culture of the day in due time. He will exalt you in strength, prove your calling and make you to fulfill your destiny. The bible says John became strong in spirit, meaning in these lonely times when you are misunderstood, and people don't want to associate with you, you will grow spiritually.

God will be speaking to you and building you up for the task ahead. When you see others enjoying themselves with their friends, you say what about me. You must know that it's God who has made you different. He has made you to hide in the deserts till the day of your showing.

You have a unique purpose, calling or destiny, and you have to separate yourself. Even if it seems like weakness or failure, you feel like you have failed to relate to others, God will exalt you and show you that it was for the good and benefit of many that you were in such a lonely state.

You don't have to feel guilty of being different. You are a leader; you are meant for great things. People may speak about you, say a lot of bad stuff but do not despair; God is with you in all that.

Mathew 11 verse 18,

For John came neither eating nor drinking, and they say he has a demon.

This was Jesus speaking about the greatness of John. He was misunderstood by the people because he was different. He couldn't conform to the society standards. He became exalted in strength after such a lonely walk in deserts with God.

Lonely times are good for you because those are times of discovery. You will discover all about yourself and what God has called you to do. You will have no disturbance because people have already given up on you and have left you alone. God will speak to you and confirm his calling upon your life. He will give you his word in such a weak season.

Luke 3 verse 2,

Annas and Caiaphas being the high priest, the word of God came unto John the son of Zachariah in the wilderness.

We see here that John was given a revelation in the lonely place of the wilderness. When it looked like a failure to relate or to do things that make you to be accepted in society, in the real sense it was successful. Hiding in weakness made John the Baptist to be exalted in strength.

It made him to be given the word about himself, who he was, and what he was to accomplish. We see that when you are lonely, despised by people, in such a time you will have clarity of your purpose. This is what being a leader is about. You will have lonely times.

You have to agree to hide in such weakness, and you will have clarity of the purpose of your leadership. John the Baptist came to the point that he had now a clear picture of God's will for his life, and he realized that he was a fulfillment of Bible prophecy.

Luke 3 verse 4,

As it is written in the book of the words of Isaiah the prophet, saying, the voice of one crying in the wilderness, Prepare the way of the Lord, make his paths straight.

So we see that it was the will of God for him to go to the wilderness, for him to be different, to be in a lonely place, in seeming failure, so that God will then exalt him in strength, and he becomes a voice calling for the preparation of the way. In such a lonely place you can come to the understanding of your gifting and the grace of God in your life.

Romans 12 verse 6,

Having then gifts differing according to the grace that is given unto us, whether prophecy, let us prophecy according to the proportion of faith.

So we see that it's about God's grace in your life. It's God who commands you to hide, be separate and; lonely sometimes, so that he gives you an understanding of your spiritual gifting. You will then have the courage to use it for the benefit of many. God makes you to know exactly who you are, your purpose in the big picture of his plan for mankind.

So when you become lonely, and see that you are not being celebrated, people don't want to associate with you, don't give up or despair, God himself will celebrate you as he shows you his plan for your life, and show you your value. Don't forget also to forgive all who were despising you, and who left you alone.

Don't hold a grudge with them; just know God was the one leading you to hide in such weakness. So when God shows you his word and a clear picture of who you are, you will be now ready to do his will. You have to start to confess positively about yourself. Speak what you know about yourself not what people are saying. People were saying John the Baptist has a demon, and he did not agree with them. Then they asked him who he was.

John 1 verse 22-23,

Then said they unto him, who are you? That we may give an answer to them that send us, what say you about yourself, He said, I am the voice of one crying in the wilderness, Make straight the way of the Lord, as said the prophet Isaiah.

So we see that this hiding in weakness was beneficial to John. It made him to change his language. It made him to start doing the will of God and not to conform to societal standards, also to start confessing positively about himself.

It seemed like a failure, but now see, it gave him confidence and courage to do God's will, and to know his purpose. So we see that when you hide in weakness, you separate yourself, and then God will exalt you in strength. So we see that John the Baptist was exalted in strength after hiding in weakness.

4. Joseph [face the test]

The meaning of hiding in Joseph's instance was that one of facing the test. It was a command to face the test, not to resist it, but to know what to do when faced with them in your journey to your destiny.

When we look at t6he story of Joseph, we can see that he did not panic when he was tested. He faced the test. That was his way of hiding in weakness. He remained silent and waited for God to intervene in his situation.

It seems like weakness or failure to remain silent when you are ignored. You know for sure that God showed you in a dream that you are going to be a ruler, and you are now using your gift to benefit others. Instead of being loved, people forget you, ignore you and don't acknowledge your gifting.

When you see this happening, you must know you are being tested. Your faith is being tested to see if you will keep on believing in that dream you saw. Joseph was ignored and forgotten for two full years, even after showing his gifting.

We know that Joseph interpreted the dreams of the baker and the butler, but afterwards, when the butler was restored to his position, he forgot about him. What was Joseph's reaction, he went on to just hide in that kind of failure, be silent and wait on God.

James 1 verse 2,

My brethren, count it all joy when you fall into various trials, knowing this, that the trying of your faith works patience, but let patience have her perfect work, that you may be perfect and entire, lacking in nothing.

So we see in this case that to HIDE in weakness is to count it all joy. It is having the knowledge that these tests are producing patience in you; they are there to make you complete and entire, lacking nothing.

God is making you to have this patience because you need it, you don't have to lack it in your destiny. In Joseph's case, the patience that was being developed in him became useful in the periods of the 7 years of plenty and 7 years of famine, when he was now Governor of Israel. He became patient enough to gather the grain in the 7 years of plenty. So this patience became a benefit to all the earth, because we can see that all the earth came to buy grain from him in Egypt in the 7 years of famine.

So we see that when the word of the Lord comes to you, there is a time when you have to hide in weakness, even when you know who you are and the purpose of your life revealed to you. In this time of hiding, God will be working in you, grooming the qualities that will be of benefit to you and the people in your destiny.

Genesis 40 verse 22,

Yet did not the chief butler remember Joseph, but forgot him.

Chapter 41 verse 1 then says, And it came to pass at the end of two full years, that Pharaoh dreamed, and behold he stood by the river. This makes us to see that Joseph spent two full years hiding in weakness, then afterwards God, then exalted him in strength when Pharaoh dreamed a dream.

The chief butler remembered him, and he interpreted the dreams of Pharaoh, and was appointed to be next in rank to Pharaoh; he became the Governor of Egypt. It was a test for Joseph to be ignored and forgotten, but we see that he passed the test. He just kept silent, faced the test, and he chose just to hide in that seeming failure, and God then exalted him in strength.

This test was a test of trust. If God is the one who showed him a dream and gave him a word that he was going to rule, he only had to trust in God fully, knowing that God's will is going to be done. Even though he was being bullied, ignored, and forgotten, God was going to intervene. His greatness was not because of his ability to make it happen, but it was all about God's ability.

Psalm 105 verse 17-21,

He sent a man before them, even Joseph, who was sold for a servant, whose feet they hurt with fetters; he was laid in irons, until the time that his word came, the word of the Lord tested him, the King sent and loosed him, even the ruler of the people, and let him go free, He made him lord of his house, and ruler of all his substance.

The above verse says until the time that his word came. This shows us that it was all timed by God. That word of Joseph becoming the ruler had its time of coming. This shows us that every word that God gives you has its time. So when you see things going the opposite direction, instead of being loved, you are forgotten, you must know that it's a test. It's only about time. You must hide in that weak season, be silent and know that the word will be fulfilled in its time.

We can see that when Joseph was now 30 years old, that became the time for him to be the ruler. God's timing is not our timing. He makes you to pass through tests for you to become mature enough for the tasks and responsibilities ahead.

1 Peter 1 verse 6,

In which you greatly rejoice, though now for a little while, if need be, you are in heaviness through manifold trials, that the trial of your faith, being much more precious than of gold that perishes, though it be tried with fire, might be found unto praise and honor, and glory at the appearing of Jesus Christ.

The above verse says if need be, you pass through trial. So if you see yourself being tried, you must know that God saw a need for you to pass through that test. God does not test you if there is no need for that test. For Joseph, there was a great need, because the perseverance that was being developed in him was going to help in the administration of the years of plenty and of famine.

This type of testing is said to be much more precious than gold. It's valuable because of what it is being used for. It's being used to make you not lack anything for the destiny in front of you. So don't try to argue or prove your point, HIDE, in that weakness of being ignored or forgotten, and then God will exalt you in strength. Face the test and in the right timing, God will give you a testimony.

5. Moses [be sent]

There is a problem in trying to do things without being sent. You can see yourself making a lot of mistakes, and you fail many times. Yes, you may have a desire to do something, but you have to HIDE in your weakness so that you will be exalted in strength as you allow God to send you.

When you now in the hiding, God will come to you, send you, and give you the authority to do it. Then you will be exalted because you will see yourself becoming successful in doing it. When God calls you and says Go, he gives you the grace to accomplish that task. You will certainly enter your destiny and fulfill your purpose.

Proverbs 3 verse 5,

Trust in the Lord with all your heart, and lean not unto your own understanding, in all your ways acknowledge him, and he shall direct your paths.

When you see yourself failing as you try to use your gifting, you must hide, create some space, allow God to be involved, read the word and wait upon him to give you direction. When you have totally surrendered it all to God, he will visit you and show you how to do it. You will therefore be exalted in strength.

When we look at the story of Moses, we can see that he made a mistake and failed as he tried to be a ruler of the Israelites. He killed an Egyptian. This was not the way God intended for him to deliver the Israelites from slavery. God had the plan at hand of how Moses was going to do it.

We see the problem of Moses, he did not wait on God, and he went on to do it with his own understanding. We see then that he did it wrong. Moses' decision after the failure is the purpose of this book.

The message is saying HIDE, in your weakness, then God will exalt you in strength. Moses made a good decision to run away to the wilderness, to just forget about leading the Israelites, to just leave it all to God. Then we see what happens, God then calls him to go after some time in the wilderness.

When God calls you now, he gives you the instructions on how to do it, and also gives you the authority to do it. You will see yourself having the courage now to enter your destiny. So we see that it's about the word of God. It's about waiting on God to call you, and you will have the strength to go forward with the purpose that he has revealed to you.

Exodus 2 verse 13-15,

And when he went out the second day, behold, two men of the Hebrews strove together, and he said to him that did the wrong, Why strike you your fellow? And he said, Who made you a prince and a judge over us, do you intend to kill me, as you killed the Egyptian? And Moses feared, and said, surely this thing is known; Now when Pharaoh heard this thing, he sought to slay Moses, but Moses fled from the face of Pharaoh, and dwelt in the land of Midian, and he sat down by a well.

We can see that when you just do your own thing without being instructed by God, you can see yourself in trouble and fail because it's not really the will of God. Yes, you may have the passion, the gift, but you have to hide, meaning you have to create space for God, wait on him.

You have to surrender it all to God, and then he will clarify it to you and tell you to go. You won't fail anymore. Although you will face challenges on the way, but you will have the assurance that God is with you. He gave you the word that he is with you all the way.

Exodus 3 verse 10-12,

Come now therefore, and I will send you unto Pharaoh, that you may bring forth my people, the children of Israel out of Egypt, And he said, Certainly I will be with you.

So we see that Moses was given the assurance of God's presence in his journey of fulfilling his purpose. This message of hiding in Moses' case was that of surrendering it all to God, for him to give you the call and send you.

If God did not say anything about what you are continually doing, you will see yourself failing. You will easily give up also because you don't have that drive to press into that destiny. So in that case, you must HIDE, meaning stop for a moment, surrender it all to God, he has a real purpose for you.

When you create space for God to act, he will visit you and call you, tell you to Go, and you will then be exalted in strength. God waits until you give up in your pursuit, then you will grow up with your understanding of his ways, then he will show up and tell you what to do. Hide in your weakness, wait for his calling, read the word of God, then you will be exalted in strength.

He will tell you exactly what you have to do, like what he did to Moses, and you then do it and fulfill your destiny. There is another aspect of moving on that you have to grasp. Yes, you know you are a leader, you have the passion and you just want to quickly make it happen. Then you see yourself making a lot of mistakes. When you see this, you have to forgive yourself, don't be too hard on yourself; move on. You will be hiding in your weakness when you decide to move on with your life.

Give yourself some time, live your life, don't hate yourself; focus on the simple things of life. It's God's will for you to have a balanced life, to grow spiritually, socially, physically, then the time will come when God will send you and give you the grace to be that leader that you wanted to be. In Moses' case, we see that he forgave himself and moved on with his life.

He went on and dwelt in the land of Midian. He married a wife from the daughters of Jethro, the priest, also had a son and he also started keeping the flock of his father in law. Then we see later that God then called him and sent him to Go, he was then exalted in strength after hiding in weakness.

6. Elijah [fellowship & worship him]

The most important thing in our lives is fellowship with God. We have to be people of praying, fasting, worshiping God, for us to be successful in all we do. God is seeking for such.

John 4 verse 23-24,

But the hour comes and now is, when the true worshipers shall worship the Father in spirit and in truth; for the Father seeks such to worship him, God is a spirit, and they that worship him must worship him in spirit and in truth.

This shows us that it's high time for us to worship God in spirit and in truth. When we are constantly working and we forget to fellowship with the Father, this will give us doubt and we see ourselves being fearful. We will fail if we do this.

When we look at the story of Elijah, we see that he was lacking fellowship with God and he became fearful when he was threatened by Jezebel then he decided to HIDE in that weakness, and then we see that God exalted him in strength when he visited him and talked to him telling him what to do next. We can see that Elijah saw his weakness and realized the need for God to intervene. He was in need of the grace of God for him to prosper.

2 Corinthians 12 verse 9-10,

And he said unto me, My grace is sufficient for you; for my strength is made perfect in weakness. Most gladly, therefore will I rather boast in my weaknesses, that the power of Christ may rest upon me. Therefore I take pleasure in weaknesses, in reproaches, in necessities, in persecutions, in distresses for Christ's sake; for when I am weak, then am I strong.

So we see that it's only by your weaknesses that God's strength is made perfect. This is because when you feel weak you see, you can't do it alone, you recognize there is need of a higher power to rest upon you for you to come out of that situation.

So we see that the weakness is there for a reason. When you take pleasure in it, you are saying okay Lord, I have seen that I'm weak, and you fellowship with him, depending entirely upon him. In this way, you are hiding in your weaknesses, and by his grace, God will show his power on you and exalt you in strength. So when you see that you are so weak, don't be depressed like Elijah and say, oh Lord kill me, because I'm weak, No, you have to realize it's only when you are weak that you are strong.

God gave you that weakness so that he uses it to show his glory. So we see that hiding in weakness, according to Elijah was going to the mount of God. It was in the form of seeking God, praying, fasting and worshiping him. It was good for Elijah to see his failure and to decide to hide by going to the mount of God. Fellowship with God is very important in your journey to fulfillment.

This is because it will lead you to receive revelation from God. He will visit you and give you instruction on the way forward. The decision of Elijah to hide in his failure and weakness is an acknowledgement that God knows more than what you know.

God knows the future, so there is need for fellowship and worship him in spirit for him to reveal to you what needs to be done. God knew the future, he knew that this Jezebel was going to perish in the time of Elisha, but Elijah did not know it. To acknowledge that wisdom is of God is to hide in the weakness of not knowing.

You hide as you seek for the all-knowing God to tell you what's going to happen. As you worship him and fellowship with him in the Holy Spirit, he will let you know the future and instruct you on the way forward. When Jezebel sends a letter to Elijah threatening him, his reaction is the message of this book. Instead of trying to use his own capability, he decided to see his weakness of not knowing.

He said I don't know about this, let me just go yonder and worship the Father who knows it all. He was saying, to the only wise God, be glory and honor both now and forevermore. His decision to HIDE in that weakness, then led him to hear the still small voice of God and he was exalted in strength.

He was then given the knowledge of what's happening and what to do next. He even thought that he was the only one left, then God made him to know that he had left seven thousand who did not bow their knee to Baal.

The problem with us most of the time is that we spent most of our time saying we know this and we know that. Knowledge and understanding belong to God. He is the only wise God. He is the one who made us to be who we are. So it's God who knows exactly what you need to do for you to fulfill your destiny.

He knows what's happening and what he has prepared already for you, for you to accomplish your task, and use your gifting for the benefit of the community. When you finally come to the conclusion that Its God who knows it all, you will HIDE in your weakness of not knowing.

You hide by going to the mount of God, fasting, worshiping and fellowshipping with him. Then when you give him the glory, he will visit you, speak to you and will exalt you in strength.

1 Kings 19 verse 4,

But he himself went a day's journey into the wilderness, and came and sat down under a juniper tree, and he requested for himself that he might die, and said, it is enough, now, O, Lord, take away my life, for I am not better than my fathers.

We see in this case that Elijah went on to hide in his weakness, he saw that he was a failure, he was lacking in knowledge and he did not know what was taking place. We can see that his choice was a good one, he chose to go into the wilderness to talk to God, to fellowship with his Master.

He decided to share his feelings and emotions with the one who cares for him through worship. We can see the benefit, God was so pleased with such an attitude that he came with a still and small voice and talked to Elijah telling him what to do. It's God's plan and will for us to come to the conclusion that we actually don't know it all. Then we worship him in the Holy Spirit, and he makes us to know. He gives us the revelation.

When we look at the conversation between Job and God, we see in Job 38 verse 4, it says, Where were you when I laid the foundations of the earth? Declare, if you have an understanding.

We see that God was making Job to see his weakness of not knowing it all, and then he repented in dust and ashes. He worshiped the only wise God, and see what happened. He was then exalted in strength and got double riches after all that trouble. So we see that you have to HIDE in your weakness of not knowing then God will exalt you in strength.

You hide by fellowship with the Father, by prayer, fasting and worshiping him; then he will be pleased with you and exalt you. You will certainly enter your destiny and fulfill your purpose. Our God is a good God.

7. Jesus [focus on fulfillment]

It's not about recognition, but it's about fulfillment. It's not about people knowing who you are, trying to show them who you are, and getting praise from them. It's about changing your focus.

You must not focus too much on getting known, but on fulfilling what God has called you to accomplish. You have to HIDE in your weakness so that you will be exalted in strength. Hiding In this case is keeping it a secret of who you are and focusing more on fulfilling the duty and task of that identity.

All your energies must be channeled in the fulfillment of what you know about yourself. So we see in this case that you will be more of a person of action, doing it, not trying to show off to people who you are.

When we look at the story of the inhabitants of Gibeon, we see that they were one of the tribes that God had assigned to the sons of Israel to destroy so that they possess the land of milk and honey. So when these people heard of how the

Israelites had destroyed the other tribes in that land, they decided to hide their real identity.

They came up with a plan. The plan was to make a covenant with the Israelites and lie that they come from a faraway place, so that they become their slaves. So we see that their plan was to keep it a secret who they really are, and to focus on fulfillment of their plan to have that covenant sealed. So we see that later when the Israelites found out that they lied, they couldn't kill them because of the covenant already sealed.

So we see that these people really focused on hiding in their weakness, and then they were exalted in strength, and became hewers of wood and drawers of water for the Israelites.

Joshua 9 verse 4,

They did work craftily, and went and made, as if they were ambassadors, and took old sacks upon their donkeys, and wine skins, and torn and mended. They then said we are come from a far country; now therefore make a covenant with us, speaking to Joshua.

We can see that they decided to hide in their weakness; they kept their real identity a secret, and focused more on fulfillment of their plan of having a covenant sealed with the sons of Israel. When it was fulfilled, then the secret was known. So we see that focusing on fulfillment worked for them.

It's about keeping it a secret who you are, and focusing on the work of fulfilling the purpose of God for your life. It seems like weakness and failure when you are not known, and your name is not on billboards, but that's not the case. You must ignore that urge to make yourself popular, its unnecessary work.

Most times people associate strength with those whose names are popular and you feel like you are not being successful. When you see this happening you must just hide in that weakness, keep your identity a secret, then focus on fulfillment of the work you were assigned to do.

The work will speak for itself. You will be exalted in strength when you have fulfilled your purpose. You will enter your destiny. So we see the best is to fill your mind with what God revealed for you to do. Focus on action, do it through the gift endowed upon you. Don't seek to be known, or to impress people, or for people praise you for who you are and what you do.

When we now look at the story of Jesus Christ, Our Lord and savior, the King of Kings, we can see that he had a great work to accomplish. He had a great purpose of the Father to fulfill. So his decision was to HIDE in his weakness of being in the form of flesh.

He focused more on fulfilling the purpose, why he came to be a man, and he said it will be known that I am the son of God after I die and rise again. His main focus was to do0 the will of his Father and to fulfill it, not to try and exalt himself to the people for them to know that he is the Christ. God chose him for the fulfillment of the redemption plan.

He was chosen to be the High Priest forever, to die for our sins, and through his blood we have forgiveness of sins, and then to rise again on the third day, to conquer death and to give us the gift of eternal life.

Hebrews 5 verse 5,

So Christ glorified not himself to be made a high priest, but he that said unto him, You are my son, today I have begotten you, as he said also in another place, You are a priest forever after the order of Melchizedek.

We see that it's God the Father who called Jesus for the fulfillment of the office of a High priest forever. He was appointed by God. He did not have to exalt himself, or try to glorify himself to be known by people. His focus became that one of fulfilling that purpose.

So we see that he decided to HIDE in his weakness of being in the form of flesh. He kept it a secret that he was the Son of God, the Christ, and just focused on doing it, and fulfilling of the task assigned to him.

Mathew 16 verse 16,

And Simon Peter answered, You are the Christ, the Son of the living God, And Jesus answered and said unto him, Blessed are you, Simon Barjona, for flesh and blood have not revealed it unto you, but my Father who is in heaven.

Then we see in verse 20, it says, Then charged he his disciples that they should tell no man that he was Jesus the Christ. This happened after Jesus asked his disciples who people said he was. So when Peter said the Christ, then he instructed them to keep it a secret. It was to be known after he rises again on the third day.

It was to be known after the covenant is sealed by his blood of us becoming forgiven of all our transgressions through his death. So we see that this fulfillment of his purpose was much more important, just like that one of the inhabitants of Gibeon. We can also see afterwards, when he was transfigured before his disciples, that he also instructed them to keep it a secret.

Mathew 17 verse 9,

And as they came down from the mountain, Jesus charged them, saying, Tell the vision to no man, until the Son of man be risen again from the dead.

Jesus Christ was glorious at the transfiguration, his face shone like the sun, but we see that he did not want that identity to be known. His decision was to hide in the weakness of his flesh by focusing more on the fulfillment of his mission on the earth. He focused more on the task he was assigned to accomplish by the Father.

He decided to keep it a secret, not to go on and tell everybody saying I am this, I am that. We see what happened after such a decision to HIDE in weakness; he was then exalted in strength. He fulfilled his purpose; he entered his destiny.

He died for our sins, and by his blood, we received forgiveness of our sins, then he rose again on the third day, and is now seated at the right hand of God the Father, with all authority, glory, and strength.

Colossians 4 verse 17,

And say to Archippus, Take heed to the ministry which you have received in the Lord, that you fulfill it.

So we see that it is all about the fulfillment of that purpose, that command of God, that task that work, and that plan of God, then you will be exalted in strength, and you will enter your destiny.

Philippians 2 verse 6-9,

Who being in the form of God, thought it not a thing to be grasped to be equal with God, But he made himself of no reputation, and took upon him the form of a servant, and was made in the likeness of men, And being in the fashion as a man, he humbled himself, and became obedient unto death, even death of the cross; Therefore God also has highly exalted him, and given him a name which is above every name, That at the name of Jesus every knee should bow, of things in heaven, and things in earth, and things under the earth, And that every tongue should confess that Jesus Christ is Lord, to the glory of God the Father.

So we see that Yes, our Lord and savior Jesus Christ was exalted in strength after hiding in weakness. This was God love shown, that every knee should bow and every tongue confess. So if you haven't confessed Jesus Christ as your personal savior, you should do it now, ask him to come into your heart, confess that Yes, you believe that he died and he rose again on the third day.

Mathew 28 verse 5-6,

And the angel answered and said unto the women, Fear not, for I know that you seek Jesus, who was crucified, he is not here, for he is risen, as he said, Come and see the place where the Lord lay.

When you do this you will be forgiven of your sins through his blood and you will have the gift of eternal life. You will certainly enter your destiny and fulfill your purpose. You then ask for the Holy Spirit to come upon you, he will reveal to you about your purpose, and give you and give you an understanding of the gifts bestowed upon you.

Then you take the decision of hiding in your weakness, and God will exalt you in strength as you depend upon him, be faithful over little, be sent, worship him and focus on the fulfillment of your purpose.

May God richly bless you and make you a blessing to many. It's because of God's love that you are now called a son of God, he is now your heavenly Father. Now we give thanks to the Father for his goodness and mercy.

CHAPTER 5

WHAT MAKES GREATNESS

[ACTION STEPS]

--Make a list of the weaknesses you are willing to fight and overcome, write down the verses from the word of God that addresses each of them, start praying and fight. [PEACE]

--Think of at least 5 ideas of how you can bless others, even those who disagree with you, start doing it [BLESSING]

INTRODUCTION

People of all works of life want to be great, worse off these days; people want popularity. Is popularity greatness, oh no, there is a very big difference. The society is fond of heroes; people have the craving to celebrate the excellence shown by one, but greatness more than expression is the impact of a given person.

SO WHAT MAKES GREATNESS is what makes an impact. The level of impact is the determining factor. So who says this is great, or who says this is not, People want to be satisfied in popularity not in changing lives. The impact is bringing about a change; a transformation,

We look at lives that made an impact, these are great lives, lives that made a change, let's take for an example, the man who invented electricity; we can all agree that was greatness. Do we have the knowledge of guessing what his focus was, popularity? Oh no, there is some hidden ingredient that makes such greatness.

In this study of mine, I came to a conclusion that greatness is a heart issue; the heart of a man reflects the man, what is inside of you. If you love to give something that impact, you don't try to get known, you try to impact, and you try by all means to see lives change for good. So the real question is, do you want to be great?

The society these days don't value greatness, they value popularity, how many people now know me, so the more they know you, is the more they will buy your product when you put it out there.

So can we say that greatness is now a thing of the past, do we not have recent examples to emulate, okay popularity is popularity, greatness is greatness.

So what makes greatness? I ask again, Impact is work, so let me speak to a few who still see lives in need and cry, wonder why, and want by all means to see a difference. They are there still, those who want to be real.

So let me write to those, tell them more of what makes that greatness, so that they increase their speed, in giving this world in need. As I see it, this world can't do without greatness, because people are in need of help, and help comes only by greatness, not by popularity searchers.

So let me spark a light to one, so that he or she will be great, and fix some part of this world which need fixing, and repair some other part which needs repairing. Let's not complain about those majorities who love to live cheap lives, and let's get to understand that one cannot only impact one but the whole world.

Those who got heart are rare, they are a gem, valuable, and we see that they are a few, an exception. Greatness is meant for all, but it is attained by a few, so I maybe speaking to that few, meant for it, so that they know what makes it.

WHAT GOD SAID IS WHAT MAKES GREATNESS

What did God say? The book called the Bible is the secret of greatness, it carries the treasure that catapults you to a life of impact, so let's dig deep into it, and see what God said….

1. PEACE

Proverbs 24 verse 27,

Make your fields ready, get prepared, and after that builds your house.

This is what makes greatness you have to get prepared first. This preparation gives you peace, and peace makes greatness.

Many people they rush to try and impact or offer something, but they still have so many issues in their lives which are still unresolved. Don't you know that those areas affect your concentration; therefore what you try to offer won't reach to greatness status because of all that.

TO BUILD SOMETHING OF IMPACT, THERE IS NEED OF REST, AND PEACE FROM MANY ENEMIES.

At that time of rest, that's when you get free to build; that's when you will really impact the society. Let's look at the Bible character called Asa, in 2 Chronicles 14, we see that he removed the pagan altars and the shrines, he smashed the sacred pillars, and cut down the Asherah poles, He commanded the people of Judah to seek the Lord, he also removed the pagan shrines as well as the incense altars from every one of Judah's towns, After this Asa's Kingdom enjoyed a period of Peace.

Then it was during this period of peace, the peaceful years that he was able to build up the fortified cities throughout Judah. For you to build something great, the principle here says, you have to be in a peaceful state. So before you say now let me go for greatness, you have to fight the enemies in your life to come to rest and peace, then you will be free to build. When you see yourself on the run and many enemies hindering you, then you know that you are not yet ready for greatness. You won't build anything of lasting impact in that state.

SO DON'T RUSH, DEAL WITH ISSUES FIRST, THAT'S WHAT GOD SAID, AND WHAT GOD SAID MAKES GREATNESS.

You can have an enemy of alcohol abuse or drug abuse, and you want to be great, fight that habit first, because it will hinder you. All the time you are in the bar drinking, and you think you can become great with such a life full of clutter; you have no rest at all.

Greatness comes with rest, you may have an enemy of unfaithfulness, deal with it, break it down, conquer it, seek the Lord and have rest first from that hindrance then you will have peace. That peace will lead to your greatness.

This is because in peaceful seasons, God will download in your heart, projects of impact. He will make you to know your gifting. Only in peacefulness does God really have work in you, and bring you to your greatness. You maybe fighting an enemy of lust deal with it first and you will be surprised when you conquer.

The universe waits for you to conquer first, to be at peace and gives you your share of greatness. Many people never became great because they ignore issues in their lives. They just rush to be popular, and try to make things happen; they don't become great because they don't prepare for it.

This principle can also be seen on those dropouts from college who make an impact, who build great products. Why dropout, you may ask them; this is mainly because of a need to be free, to have rest and peace. Free to build, some of them will tell you that dropping out was the best move because it gave them peace. It got them free to build something of lasting impact. So we see that they got rid of something first for them to reach for greatness, that's the principle, that's what God said in Proverbs; it makes greatness.

When we look at the Bible character called David, we see that it was in his heart to build a Temple for God, but God refused him to have a share in that greatness. We hear God saying to David, no, you are a man of war; your son will build me a house, because he will be a son of peace and rest. In that season of rest from all enemies, Solomon your son is going to build me the Temple.

So we see that David was the one who fought all the battles and won against all enemies first, and after that the land was at peace. Then Solomon comes in that season of peace, and he builds the Temple of the Lord.

This is the principle to greatness, you have to get prepared first, make yourself ready, and then you will build something of lasting impact. You need to have a free mind, a mind not cluttered with many things. This is a mind that can focus and do excellent things that will benefit many.

2. LOVE

Okay, still on what God said; first we said God said peace makes greatness, now we see also that God said love makes greatness.

WHOSE LOVE, HIS LOVE MAKES GREATNESS…

John 19 verse 4,

Understand clearly that I find him not guilty.

God finds you not guilty. When he gives you an opportunity to do something of an impact, he finds you not guilty. This is because many of the times you deal with enemies in your life, Yes, you got rid of this and that, you now have peace. But as you try to act, you see accusations coming to hinder you from your pursuit of greatness. These accusations come in various forms, to cause depression, pain and make you suffer.

They try to frustrate your mission to greatness, but we now see that the answer to those accusations is God himself who will find you not guilty, and he shows his love, love, love to you. This is what makes greatness. The Bible says in Psalms 109 verse 28, They may curse, but you will bless, when they attack, they will be put to shame, but your servant will rejoice, My accusers will be clothed with disgrace and wrapped in shame as in a cloak.

Because you are aiming for greatness, you will surely have enemies. So what makes greatness is only the Love of God, who will bless when many are pronouncing curses on you. When we look at the verse again we see the man called Jesus, who was accused, beaten, given pain, and was given the crown of thorns, So what made Jesus great, it was only the Love of God.

This is because we know God had already spoken about him, saying, You are a High Priest forever, you are going to die and on the third day rise again.

So after all those accusations, they killed him, and God's love proved him not guilty, and made him to rise again on the third day, then he was made great, and he made a huge impact to the world. This is because he died to save humanity from sin through his blood, and many who now believe in him are given eternal life. Now we divide him a portion with the great as Prophet Isaiah says; because he was numbered with the transgressors.

So we see that what makes greatness is what God said, When God says you are not guilty, he will be showing his love for you. When you are being accused it hinders you, slows you down, and it maybe be a very painful experience, but be cheerful because God comes into the picture and says not guilty. He opens doors for you to be of impact to the society; this makes greatness. Love makes greatness.

Look at the other Bible character called Joseph, we can see that he was accused, put in prison, but what happened next, God found him not guilty by giving him an opportunity in the prison to use his gift of interpreting dreams. Then he was released to interpret the dreams of Pharaoh, and then he became great, and was promoted to become the Governor next in rank to Pharaoh

SO WE SEE THAT WHAT MAKES GREATNESS IS NOT MORE OF YOUR EFFORT BUT THE LOVE OF GOD, WHO SAYS YOU ARE NOT GUILTY, AND HE PROVES IT BY GIVING YOU AN OPPORTUNITY TO BE AN IMPACT…

He also blesses you when many are cursing you. For God is a God of justice, he says not guilty; he is a God of love, love, love. This makes you great. So all you have to do is get to his side, give your life to him, and surrender your life. When you are now on his side, he will defend you, and say you are not guilty, and bless you to make an impact. He will reveal to you your greatness; show you what you do to be of great impact to the world at large

Romans 8 verse 33,

Who will bring any charge against those whom God has chosen? It is God who justifies; it is God who says not guilty,

So what makes greatness is what God says. He says not guilty and creates an opportunity for you to use the gifting he put inside of you, and makes you an impact. Those who were accusing you and making you suffer will be ashamed. This is what makes Greatness.

3. BLESSING

Now we also see that after you deal with enemies inside of you, and you have peace, God then deals with enemies outside you as he shows you Love, you now come to a stage where you have to bless those enemies in the contrary. That makes Greatness. It's the other thing that God said; we are still on what God said mind you.

GREATNESS COMES WHEN YOU DO THINGS ON THE CONTRARY; WHEN YOU DO THE OPPOSITE OF WHAT'S EXPECTED, INSTEAD OF RETURNING EVIL WITH EVIL, YOU RETURN WITH BLESSING…

You have knowledge that you are called to greatness, you are called to bless, and you continue to bless even in a world that is so cold. You are there to make it warm.

1 Peter 3 verse 9,

Do not return evil for evil, but on the contrary bless, for to this you have been called so that you inherit a blessing.

This is what God said, and it makes Greatness.

It's when you do what's not expected from somebody who was accused countless times. You see it as an opportunity to bless. You bless the world by making use of your gifting; be it giving out a product or a service, forgetting the accusations, ignoring the pain, just acting and blessing instead. When you do this, you are now a candidate of Greatness.

Let's look at Joseph, see what he did to his brothers who accused him, who did evil to him by selling him to the Egyptians. He blessed them instead; that's greatness. He understood his calling, which all I have to do is bless. Then we see what happened next, he became great; the whole earth came to buy grain from him at the time of famine, he fed the whole earth. This is because of his attitude of just blessing others, on the contrary.

Many people when they face opposition, they stop doing good, they stop thinking of ideas to be an impact or to bless, but no, that's not what makes greatness. What makes greatness is what God said, God said just bless, and you are called for it.

Opportunity to bless will come when you have that mentality, of being a blessing to all, even to those who were discouraging you. So we see that this principle makes greatness, it makes you stay motivated, stay passionate, and stay with the zeal, even in painful situations. You become great as you bless, and bless even more.

4. SEPARATION

Still on what God said, now let's get to the fourth thing. We can see that Separation makes Greatness. God said it, and it makes you great.

2 Corinthians 6 verse 17,

Therefore, come out from them and separate yourselves from them, says the Lord, don't touch their filthy things, and I will welcome you, and I will be your Father, and you will be my sons and daughters, says the Lord Almighty.

This is another principle that makes Greatness.

YOU HAVE TO BE SEPARATE SO THAT YOU WILL BE DIFFERENT FROM ALL, THIS MAKES YOU GREAT…

This is because most of the time if you stay with the society, you will take the language of the society, this will limit you. What makes greatness is separation. In lonely times, that's where God will show the right thing to do, will give you ways of showing love to the world. God will give revelation of your purpose, and the impact you can make. This comes only when you are separate without hindrance from the environment.

The very thing that hinders greatness is familiarity. People in a community want to tell each other what to do, they give each other clues about how far one can go, this will limit you, and it makes many people settle for mediocrity. But when you dare to stand alone, you will do great exploits. This is because you will be free to follow what God will be directing you to do.

CHAPTER 6

YOUR GREATNESS IS IN 7 WORK ENVIRONMENTS [I.T.H.R.I.V.E]

[ACTION STEPS]

--Make a plan of how you are going to use the latest technology in your greatness pursuit, then switch that plan into action. [TECHNOLOGY]

--Write down ways in which you can best interact with others, join a club, and open a social network account. [INTERACTIVE]

--Make a list of the organizations that you think have a vision that lines with yours, then volunteer your efforts, join the team, or just try to connect in any way. [VISION DRIVEN]

1. INTERACTIVE

Communication is key to your greatness, so an environment of more interaction contains your greatness. Information sharing is what makes some companies to be great. This is because the more information you have, the more better you are in decision making.

Great companies are saving a lot of dollars and cutting unnecessary expenses as they interact with others in their business endeavors. As you interact with different suppliers, you can see different prices for certain parts in your production chain, this will help you to reduce wastage. You can then easily negotiate for a reduction because of that information.

So we see that an interactive environment has greatness attached to it. In the Bible, David interacted with others and got the information that the person to kill Goliath was going to be given the daughter of the King. That information affected his decision making. He decided to act and fight that Philistine. Yes, he became great because of such environment.

So you must stay in such an environment for you to be great. Information is success; you need to know, so the sharing of information is the best to make greatness. Information sharing creates confidence. When you know something, you will have no doubt, and this will make you move to your greatness.

2. TECHNOLOGY

Greatness is found by those who adapt to the latest technologies. The world is changing, and technology is picking its pace. So for you to be of value, you have to get in line, Adapt, take it and use it, be in such an environment.

These days are days of smartphones and other devices that are increasing the efficiency in doing things. Don't be negative about these changes. You will limit your impact, and you will reduce your chances of becoming great.

Greatness comes by advancing your way of doing things through the use of all these technologies.

ECCLESIASTES 10 verse 10-

Skill helps one to succeed

Be skillful through the use of latest technologies, this contains your greatness.

3. HUMOROUS

Are the people around you, always negative and not smiling? Are they enjoying the work they are doing? If not, this type of environment does not contain your greatness. It's a hindrance.

You must stay in a place where people have joy in their hearts. Having joy does not mean you are playing around with your work or gifting, it just means you enjoy it, and you have a lot of passion.

Your greatness is contained in a place where people have a victorious attitude. This allows you to use your imagination. A fun place is a place of imagination, and imagination is the seed to your greatness. Freeing your spirit is what leads to great inventions.

So a moody place has no freedom at all, great ideas die with such moods. Even customers they can shun a salesperson who tries to sell their products in a moody way. It shows that he/she is not even sure of his offer, so how can you wish to impact another if you yourself are not impacted.

4. REACHING OUT

An environment where people reach out to the community contains your greatness. Socially responsible companies are great. Greater love has no man than this, to lay down your life for your brethren, Jesus said.

The mark of greatness is in giving, so if you stay in such a place, you will become great for sure. Giving a helping hand affects you in a positive way, so such an environment is of much benefit to you. You will also look for ways to help shape the society, and this will lead to your greatness.

5. INITIATIVE

An environment that promotes creativity contains your greatness. Creativity is the essence of greatness. A work environment that challenges you to come out with ideas can impact you in a positive way.

You will discover your potential. It stretches your mind and makes you great. Look at Joseph in the Bible; pharaoh needed his dreams to be interpreted. An environment with such motivation to be creative can move you to act and become great.

Joseph became a great man as he interpreted the dreams of Pharaoh. So you must stay in such a place, a place of possibility. Your idea might change the world, and your gift might touch countless lives. You will become great.

6. VISION DRIVEN

This environment is where people see far; it contains your greatness. Without a vision, the people perish, the Bible says. When you stay in such a place, you will bounce back from defeat. You will persevere because you are staying with people who have the future in mind.

It increases your determination to make it, so therefore makes you great. The fuel to greatness is determination. It only comes with vision driven people.

They don't give up because they have seen where they are going to end up at. Such a place is where you must stay, and surely you will become great as you associate with such caliber of people.

7. EVER-COMPETITIVE

This environment promotes Greatness. This is because it challenges you to work hard, to do more and to be more. It's an environment of people with a global view. Global business is highly competitive. If you have this focus, you will always be on the road to improve your products so that they can match with the standards.

This global focus type of environment contains your greatness. As you work hard to match with others in the international arena, you will discover your greatness. You will know your skill and strength, and you will surely be great. Let's look at the Global view in greater detail in the next chapter.

CHAPTER 7

THE GLOBAL VIEW—WALKING WITH GOD IS RAISING THE STANDARDS

[ACTION STEPS]

---Write down ways in which you can turn your business into the international arena, and start acting on them.

---Create a website for your business, product, service, ministry or work.

---Make sales calls to international dealers, license your brand internationally.

---Connect to international players in the industry you are in.

INTRODUCTION

Somebody is with his family in a Hotel, and it has many people in it, about a thousand. Suddenly he has a revelation, and he starts to speak with his family. Somebody in the family says, Yes, Daddy has so much passion. Then daddy grabs the Mick, oh no, people start to say, you can't do that, and then the daddy refuses to stop. He starts speaking now through the Mick, guess what happens, all in that hotel starts hearing that message, then he says; Walking with God is raising the standards, and he starts to explain what he means.

He says, the moment I took this Mick, I'm raising the standards, because now I'm not teaching my family only, but I'm now impacting a thousand people; that's a sign of walking with God.

God is in the Highest Heavens, so his view and our view are different. He sees from a high level. When you see from a high level, things become smaller and small; you will see the whole world as a small sphere. That's how God sees, so walking with such a God makes you change your focus. You will see that it's possible to impact many.

LUKE 18 verse 27

What is impossible with man is possible with God.

So when you walk with God, you will get God's view of ministry or business, you will not be comfortable with being a local hero anymore. You will start to explore with courage, the whole world type of impact. This will make you great.

Bear in mind that people in your local place will say to you, what are you trying to do, you won't make it, stop, but in this book I'm saying don't stop. You are walking with God, you have a different view.

PSALM 2 verse 8

Ask of me, and I will make the nations your inheritance, the ends of the earth your possession.

That is a true promise, and God desires that for you; to impact globally. Asking shows that you are talking, so we see that when you are walking with someone, there is communication involved. That's why we saw that great daddy suddenly grabbing the Mick; this is because he has been speaking with God. So God told him about many people, not just his family. So now he decides to act on it. That is walking with God; it's when you act in faith according to his will, God will be pleased with you.

When you speak with God, you will see as God sees; he sees from the highest view. He sees the whole world.

So we see what walking with God is; its raising the standards, having a Global view, going an extra mile with faith and courage on your convictions. Let's see different biblical characters that were walking with God, and see how they raised their standards, impacted on a Global scale, and became great.

1. ABRAHAM

Abraham is the example of a man who was walking with God; we see that even his name was changed by God from Abram to Abraham, meaning you are now a father of many nations. His view got changed to a Global one. So if you begin to walk with God in your business or ministry, you will change, even you brand name to fit your Global focus. Your brand name must show that you are walking with a God that sees afar not just local.

You must escape with courage from your local, family confinement, because that is a limitation to you. You are a child of the most High God.

GENESIS 12 verse 1-3

The Lord said to Abraham-Leave your country, your people, and your family's household and go to the land I will show you, I will make you a great nation, and I will bless you, I will make your name great, and you will be a blessing, I will bless those who bless you, and whoever curses you, I will curse. And all the people of the earth will be blessed through you.

We can see that Abraham left as God had told him, he obeyed. He raised his standard as he walked in faith to a land of promise. To walk with God is to see differently, you can only see differently when you have a revelation. You must see as God sees. God talked to Abraham about all the people of the earth. That is a type of impact that God saw in this man. It only came in communication with God.

So we see that God is the only wise God, he is all knowing; he knows what he is doing. When you walk with God, he will change your view.

God will make you change your brand identity; you will be blessed and will become a blessing to many. His plans are different from ours, even his thoughts.

ISAIAH 55 verse 8-9,

For my thoughts are not your thoughts, neither are your ways my ways, declares the Lord, As the heavens are higher than the earth, so are my ways higher than your ways, and my thoughts than your thoughts.

God thinks higher things for us, his ways are higher, so if you dare to stand and raise the standard through global thinking, it's a sign that you are walking with God. We can see that in our business circles, some have gone all the way by including 'international' as part of their brand identity, to add international after your name, shows that you are doing your business or ministry on a global scale. That is rising of the standard.

Even the quality of your products or services will be of high standards, because of your focus. So I encourage you to rise, and take your position, see many people. Focus is everything; the only reason for most failures is wrong focus.

But if you do it in a spiritual way, pray and worship, communicate with God, your focus becomes clear; you will be walking with God. Your view will change, you will begin to think as God thinks, you will think globally, then your standard will be raised, and you will never be the same again.

2. JOSEPH

This other time I was praying and worshiping the Lord, and the Holy Spirit said to me, do not fret, the anointing is for the benefit of all, look at Joseph. Okay, I began to study about Joseph, and to know more about what happened to him. I discovered that Joseph was walking with God. A sign of his walk with God was the raising of the standards; he went from being just a mere servant of one of Pharaoh's officials to a Governor of Egypt, and became a very great man.

There is a statement that says start small, yes, we agree, but please don't stay small. When you walk with God, he will let you know this; that you are not meant for small things, you are meant to impact millions of people around the world, with products or service or ministry. God said to me, the anointing is for all; meaning all the earth. As we look at Joseph, we can see that he benefited all the earth. There was a famine in the whole world, and the whole world came to buy bread from Joseph.

GENESIS 41 verse 57

And all the countries came to Egypt to buy grain from Joseph, because the famine was severe in all the world.

So we see that this was God's view of impact of Joseph. God was seeing all the world getting fed through him. Joseph was faithful in serving in a small way, but the anointing in him was meant for Global impact. We can see that God gives direction through opportunity when you walk with him.

Joseph's opportunity came after he used his gifting locally in the jail. He helped to interpret the dreams of the baker and cupbearer. Then after that Pharaoh had a dream which needed interpretation. This was no longer small; it was now involving the whole world. This was greatness at its best.

When you walk with God, your success will not be limited, you will raise the standards. This is because of God's view; it is on another level, its high, so it involves many people. Just like the dream of the daddy who decides to hold the Mick, you must also make that decision. Decide to see the opportunity, to grab it, and to move to impact on a global scale. The Mick was an instrument that he used for the benefit of many.

This shows us that you have to open your eyes and see the opportunity, use the instruments that are there in this day and age. The opportunities are endless because of these recent technologies, like the internet, television, social media, and smart phones. Your impact on a global scale is just a click away.

So all you have to do is rise and take it, raise the standards of your business, or your ministry, or your work, by connecting globally. Don't listen to the word that says don't go, you have to go for it, you will impact millions, and you will become great. That's being wise; it takes wisdom to survive and to be successful.

ECCLESIASTES 10 verse 10

Skill will help one to succeed, -wisdom helps

A sign that you are walking with God is having wisdom. Your standard is raised through wisdom. When we look at Joseph, we can see that he knew exactly what to do. This is because the Spirit of the Lord was with him. He came up with a plan of what to do in the 7 years of plenty; the plan of saving food. We hear Pharaoh, saying, can we find anyone like this man, one in whom is the Spirit of God. Then he was put in charge, and we see that he impacted on a Global scale.

An encouragement to walk with God is an encouragement to seek after him, trust him, pray, and worship him, then be filled with the Holy Spirit. God will begin to do big things with you not small. You will have a world view. As you will open your eyes and see the need, then God gives you the grace to offer help internationally as you meet the need, in this way you will be raising the standards.

3. ENOCH

Enoch is the man that we here in the bible that walked with God, and what happened to him next was great. We hear that he did not die, he was taken by God.

GENESIS 5 verse 24

Enoch walked with GOD, and then he was no more, because God took him away.

Every step that Enoch took was a step Higher; therefore God took him to the Highest Heavens. I want to relate this story to our business, ministry or work, and say, we must be no more, no more to lower standards of doing things. If you move with God, you are moving with the times, don't stay there on lower levels of impact, No, rise. Take a step Higher, be not found; erase the local mentality, and be not found in that state of thinking, then you will move higher to a level of Global impact, and greatness.

It's not easy to just change your focus and start to act on a global scale, that's a land of the unknown. You have to persist, and to persevere. You have to study on how you can impact internationally. Don't give up, local is easy, but international seem like a great mountain to move, but if you are moving with God, he is the helper for your standards to rise.

PROVERBS 4 verse 18

The path of the righteous is like the first gleam of dawn, shining ever brighter till the full light of day.

This is how people who walk with God shine; they move to higher standards, they shine ever brighter. When you have a global view, and you are righteous, it's a sign that you are walking with God. God is a holy God. We can go back to Enoch; we can see that he was a holy man of God. So for you to be of greater impact, you need to be righteous. Shun evil, and you will impact on your business, ministry or work endeavors. Evil behavior is a hindrance. Your dreams won't come true if you are living in sin.

PROVERBS 13 verse 19

It is pleasant to see dreams come true, but fools will not turn from evil to attain them.

This shows us that dreams are attained by those who shun evil. When you see a person's dreams coming true, and he or she becoming a global impact player in an industry, you can definitely know that they are walking with God. You can know that they are shunning evil. To walk with a God who dwells on the most High place, requires you also to be holy, and your dreams will come true; you will raise the standards of your business, ministry or work.

Going back to Enoch, we can see that he was talked about again in the Bible as we relate to the issue of shunning evil to attain your dreams.

JUDE 14

Enoch, the seventh from Adam, prophesied about these men; See, the Lord is coming with thousands upon thousands of his holy ones, to judge everyone and to convict all the ungodly of all the ungodly acts they have done in the ungodly way, and all the harsh words ungodly sinners have spoken against him, These men are grumblers and faultfinders, they follow their own evil desires, they boast about themselves and flatter others for their own advantage.

So we see that Enoch was a righteous man, his standards were raised because of that. He saw thousands upon thousands. He saw with the eyes of God, just because he was walking with God. His view was altered to a higher one. He saw millions of holy ones. This made him to prophecy about the judgment of the evil. He saw the Global scale of God's plan. God has compassion for many to be numbered among the Holy ones, and many to escape the wrath to come.

Walking with GOD is rising of the level of compassion. DON'T just look at your local area and see people in need of help. When you walk with God, you will be transformed in heart; you will have the heart of God. He feels for millions around the world. You will not settle for less. As Enoch started to feel for millions, and he was not, God took him. He raised the standards; he went to a higher level.

The product you are selling, why do you want to stay in a local retail store, Give it away, license it to the big guys who will make it go Global. That machine that you invented, why do you want to keep it to yourself, to keep it on the local place, give it up; that idea is meant for the whole world. You will surely become great if you do this.

Change your view; that's a sign of walking with God. God did not give you that idea for a few local people, it must benefit the world. Feel for the world at large. It's a heart transformation you need.

Take that step, see thousands upon thousands like Enoch, and you will be no more to the small minded, you will not be found among those. You will become great and your standards will be raised to a higher level. That ministry is meant to impact millions, so step up, and raise the standards of ministry.

Change your focus to the Global type. Many souls are waiting for you. You have it in you; you are already empowered for millions around the world. Don't trip away to obscurity; you are walking with the Most High God.

4. PAUL

2 CORINTHIANS 10 verses 15-16

Neither do we go beyond our limits by boasting of work done by others, our hope is that, as your faith continues to grow, our area of activity among you will greatly expand, so that we can preach the gospel in the regions beyond you, For we do not want to boast about work already done in another man's territory.

Paul's desire and hope was to go beyond, to move up, and to raise the standards of ministry. This should be your desire in your business, or ministry. We can see Paul in Acts moving to different regions, and countries, from Jerusalem, to Rome to Spain. This was mainly because he was walking with God. Walking with God makes you to change your agenda, your aim or mission statement so that it includes the whole world.

The book of Acts is associated with the Holy Spirit. We can see that the Apostles started their walk with God as they received the Holy Spirit. It came mightily upon them with an agenda; The agenda was for greater standards of impact. It was for Global witnessing.

ACTS 1 verse 8

But you will receive power when the Holy Spirit comes on you, and you will be my witnesses in Jerusalem, and in all Judea and Samaria, and to the ends of the earth.

For sure that promise was fulfilled, the Holy Spirit came in its mighty force, and we see the disciples moving from their local areas to the whole earth. Paul was one of those who also got anointed with the Spirit, and he began his missionary journeys, and started to witness around the world.

So my question is, are you boasting of that little achievement, of that little store that you opened in your local area. You must go beyond that, look to other territories, have the view of the Spirit; that's a sign that you are walking with God.

Don't be satisfied with your own limitation. Be like Paul, who started to look beyond, to hope for more. You should also learn about the cultures and behaviors of other nations for you to be of impact to them. To have a global view of ministry or business or work takes a lot of research and study.

You should have an understanding of the cultural heritage of those nations, so that you can be of impact. This is what greatness is all about. It's all about winning; in ministry you win souls, in business, you have to win customers. So a sign that you are walking with the Most High God is when you win, when you move from winning less, or local to winning international.

You must familiarize with the languages of the nations to win. The Spirit of GOD that came upon these people like Paul was a Spirit that familiarized with the languages of the world. This was a show of its agenda.

So when the Spirit came mightily upon these disciples, their standards were raised. They started to speak in different languages of the nations. Their impact became Global; for God's concern is for nations not just a few people.

ACTS 2 verse 1-13

When the day of Pentecost came, there were all together in one place, Suddenly a sound like the blowing of a violent wind came from Heaven and filled the whole house where they were sitting, they saw what seemed to be tongues of fire that separated and came to rest on each of them, all of them were filled with the Holy Spirit, and began to speak in other tongues as the Spirit enabled them.

Now there were staying in Jerusalem God-fearing Jews from every nation under heaven, when they heard this sound, a crowd came together in bewilderment, because each one heard them speaking in his own language, utterly amazed, they asked, Are not these men who are speaking Galileans? Then how is it that each of us hears them in his own native language? Parthians, Medes, and Elamites, residents of Mesopotamia, Judea, and Cappadorcia, Pontus and Asia, Phrygia and Pamphlia, Egypt and the parts of Libya near Cyrene, visitors from Rome [both Jews and converts to Judaism], Cretans and Arabs-we hear them declaring the wonders of God in our own tongues, amazed and perplexed, they asked one another, what does this mean, some, however made fun of them and said, they have had too much wine.

This is the same amazement that must happen to you to show that you are walking with God. People must be surprised as you raise your standards. They must say, what is this, you are now impacting different nations and languages with your products, services, inventions, ministry or work.

We see that the Holy Spirit came with its own standards of service and doing of things. It introduced people to Global scale type of witnessing as disciples started to speak in all languages of the world.

Walking with God is walking with the Holy Spirit, and the view of the Spirit also becomes your view. The Spirit sees all nations. He sees the whole world in need, so suddenly your view changes, you will not be limited no more, and this will surprise many. People knew you as just a local hero.

As people were saying these are just Galileans, what has happened to them, they also say the same to you. Just as that daddy we talked about earlier, as he was now holding the Mick, many were amazed, and surprised, saying, what is this, he is now speaking to many people. That was raising of the standards at its best. It happens because of Walking with the Most High God.

5. JESUS CHRIST

When you are walking with the Highest God, he will speak and declare higher things about your life. So all you have to do is to say Amen to that word. Just say, so be it Father according to your will; agree with God and so you will be established. You must know that the word of God will surely remain. It will do what it was sent to do, its eternal.

LUKE 21 verse 33

Heaven and earth will disappear, but my words will remain forever

The words of God, will last. So you must change your confession, that's another sign that you are walking with God, this will make your standards to be raised. You will see what you were talking about come to pass.

When we look at Jesus Christ of Nazareth, we see that he was ministering at a local level, healing the sick, casting out demons. BUT his declarations were showing that he was walking with God, because he spoke of saving the whole world.

LUKE 18 verse 31-34

Jesus took the twelve aside, and told them, We are going to Jerusalem, and everything that is written by the Prophets about the Son of Man will be fulfilled, He will be handed over to the Gentiles, They will mock him, insult him, spit on him, flog him and kill him, on the third day he will rise again. The disciples did not understand any of this, its meaning was hidden from them and they did not know what he was talking about.

So what are you saying about your business? Begin to confess of impacting the whole world and that will be a sign that you are walking with God. Even if local people, your family and others do not understand you, keep speaking it, and it will be established. Speak Globally. Greatness comes through your confessions.

You not only have to see as God sees, but you must also speak as God speaks. We can also see Jesus saying his words came from the Father, to show us that he was speaking the words of God when he talked about impacting the whole world.

JOHN 14 verse 24

These words you hear are not my own, they belong to the Father who sent me.

Jesus was in the habit of speaking his international impact. He was declaring it, that he was going to die, and by his blood the whole world was going to be forgiven of all their transgressions, and he was going to rise again on the third day.

We see afterwards that it happened as he confessed. He died and rose again on the third day, and by his blood, we are forgiven of all our transgressions, and we are given the gift of eternal life, we are now blessed people in this world and the world to come.

You just now have to confess, and believe, so you will be saved, Say, Lord Jesus Christ, come into my heart, and be my Lord and Savior, I believe that you died and rose again on the third day for me to live, forgive me of my sins, from now on I am a child of the Most High God, thank you Father, in Jesus Christ's name, Amen

Now we see that God did his work with Jesus, he will also do his work with you. Agree with him, speak it, and declare that you are meant for World service, you are meant to help millions around the world, and you will see the difference. You will become great.

What you say is what you get, what you talk about is what comes to you. Be brave, and advance globally, through the words you speak. You will raise the standards of your ministry, business, and work as you follow the example of our Lord and Savoir Jesus Christ—That will be a sign that you are Walking with the Most High God.

www.ingramcontent.com/pod-product-compliance
Lightning Source LLC
Chambersburg PA
CBHW070118080526
44586CB00013B/1325